Ask The Experts:

How Did
YOU
Get A Bar Job?

If YOU don't Entertain Your Customers… Someone Else will!
Give Customers a Reason
To Come To Your Bar,
Stay Longer,
Spend More Money,
Tip Well,
and
Tell All Their Friends
What A Great Time They Had.
**Treat Every Customer As If They Have
10,000 Twitter Followers."** - Myers Barnes

Author - Scott Young Founder of: Bar Smart Inc.
www.ExtremeBartending.Com
www.TheBartendingMasters.Com
www.NightclubBarAndRestaurantTraining.Com
www.MixedDrinkRecipes.Net

Scott Young and Bar Smart Inc. ©2016

authorHOUSE®

AuthorHouse™
1663 Liberty Drive
Bloomington, IN 47403
www.authorhouse.com
Phone: 1 (800) 839-8640

Published by AuthorHouse   11/09/2016

ISBN: 978-1-5246-4890-9 (sc)
ISBN: 978-1-5246-4889-3 (e)

Library of Congress Control Number: 2016918648

Print information available on the last page.

Any people depicted in stock imagery provided by Thinkstock are models, and such images are being used for illustrative purposes only.
Certain stock imagery © Thinkstock.

This book is printed on acid-free paper.

Because of the dynamic nature of the Internet, any web addresses or links contained in this book may have changed since publication and may no longer be valid. The views expressed in this work are solely those of the author and do not necessarily reflect the views of the publisher, and the publisher hereby disclaims any responsibility for them.

www.NightclubBarAndRestaurantTraining.Com

"Every Man I Meet Is Superior To Me In Some Way

And In That,

I Shall Learn From Him."

- Ralph Waldo Emerson

Life Doesn't Always Give Second Chances,

Take The First One.

James A. Jenkins

- LastCallBartenders4Hire.com

Legal Notices and Disclaimer
As much as I'd love to think that every reader of this book will follow its advice and become fabulously wealthy by result, the truth is that I can't promise that will happen for you.

I can't guarantee that you will actually read the book or follow our suggestions. I wish I could, but I can't.
So here's the nitty-gritty legal statement:

THERE IS SO MUCH TO LEARN FOR EVERY LEVEL OF SERVICE GIVER

I hope you use this valuable and truly one of a kind "Tool" to help keep you motivated & excited to get bar every night for many years to come.

**Thank you to over 200 experts who
contributed to this series of books.**

You will get to know them as you read it because everyone has been given full credit for their thoughts and insights into being an exceptionally successful individual as a bartender.

As you will soon see, these many books represent not just my life's work, 26 years so far in the hospitality industry, but also **snapshots of wisdom from 200 other Seasoned Pros, Authors and Bar Trainers.**

(Read more about this in – Scott Interviews The Experts – Who Are They?)

Through in-depth and non-censored Interviews
on
11 important topics and writings
from
their books and/or magazine articles
they have shared much of their experience
and written content with me
so I can continue to help increase
the level of professionalism in the industry that we all love so much.

Our guests and industry are changing
and evolving all the time,
we should too.

Read with your mind open to considering
new ways to look at your profession
and you will
create a path that is uniquely your own.

Good Luck to you – Scott Young ☺

**We Are All "Service Givers"
and
"Memory Makers."**

TABLE OF CONTENTS

"Just Make Up Your Mind At The Very Outset

That Your Work Is

Going to Stand For Quality,

That You Are Going to Stamp a Superior Quality

Upon Everything That Goes Out Of Your Hands,

That Whatever You Do

Shall Bear the Hallmark of Excellence."

- Orison Swett Marden

AUTHOR'S NOTE

 Hi, My name is Scott and I'll be your friendly neighborhood author and instructor ☺

I am completely on your side and want you to succeed HUGE!

Don't be afraid to try new things. That's exactly what we want and expect from pros like you, so make the most of the time, training resources and opportunities that you have.

I'm not just a guy who has done a bit of research and written a book/s.
I've actually lived the life behind the bar for 26 years, traveled around the world teaching, learning and performing.

I have succeeded and failed over and over and over again. I've taught myself to not be afraid to ask questions, even really basic and maybe obvious or even "stupid" ones.

I've asked a lot of questions and I know some people have thought I was a bit slow sometimes for asking them. I DON'T CARE. ☺ I'm not in high school anymore where I was sometimes intimidated and I didn't ask the questions I should have. Who did it hurt? Only me. I'm not that kid anymore.

That's why I'm qualified to write these books and offer you suggestions to improve your job/career.

I've actually been there and done that and I've done it over and over again. I've experimented and wrote down my results. I'm not perfect by a long shot and there are going to be things I suggest that won't work in your type of venue or for your personality. That's okay, if you keep an open mind you will find lots of strategies and tips that will apply to you.

*** **Do not be intimidated** by how much content is in this book and series of books.
There is no way you can read and/or assimilate all of it in a day or even a week etc.

It is intended to be an in depth, encyclopedia of knowledge for you to have and to utilize for your entire career.

Make The Most of This Opportunity.

- Take lots of notes on comments, ideas and sections that "Resonate" with you
- Write the pages that interest you the most so you can come back to them later and really read everything about it.

About The Author
I feel strongly that if you're being trained by us, you have the right to know about my life, experiences and accomplishments etc.

Why? Have you ever read a book by someone claiming to know something but they don't really tell you much about themselves or their credentials?

That really frustrates me!! How do you judge the value of their suggestions?
Do they really know what they're talking about?

You have the right to really get to know the author.
Or at least be reassured that I know what I'm talking about and how I got here.

Scott's Bio – Go to… www.TheBartendingMasters.Com/MeetTheExperts (Some of the story below)

All Servers
Are Definitely
Not
Created Equal

When you choose the service industry as a career, like any other job or career, you will find that all servers are not created equal. There is a very wide range of people and their approaches out there.

Some people are passionate about being the best and some just do it as a means to live and kind of "coast" by their shifts and careers.

This isn't a very politically correct thing to say, but there are a lot of servers etc. out there that just plain suck! :)

That's right I said it. I want to be clear… I'm not saying this because I think I am so great, I don't believe that I'm god's gift to bartending or the service industry by any stretch of the imagination... Oh, the mistakes I've made! :-) I tell you about some of them in this series.
No one is perfect and we all make mistakes.

Yes, I'm a pretty good bartender and service giver and I have done very well. The reason that I think so many servers are not very good, really boils down to one thing:

They Don't Care Enough, To Think About How To Do Their Job Better.

Well I do care, and so should you!
I have spent an enormous amount of time over my 26 years in the bar industry thinking about how to be an exceptional service giver and bartender.

On top of that, I actually took action.
I began experimenting with different ways to do things, say things, and handle common situations.
"Plan Your Work, Work Your Plan"

I have created a game plan that helped me increase my odds of success and it's all here for you.

Why make the effort?…
Effort? Aw man, that sounds like work…

Hehe, sometimes it is, especially in the beginning when you're learning something new or just changing how you have always done something. This isn't a get-rich-in-30-days program.
You are not "entitled" to make huge money and not do anything for it.

But I promise you, if you follow my suggestions, it will be well worth your while.
In money made, pure enjoyment of your time behind the bar, opportunities and pride of a job well done.

I've followed this strategy and that has helped me succeed at a very high level, which means;
- I was offered the best bartending job in my city,
- I was given the best bar shifts
- I had really high sales
- I made fantastic amounts of Tips
- I had tons of fun being a bartender, every night I "worked"

If you do it right, I think bartending is the best job in the world.
Being a table server is a lot of fun too, but I only did it occasionally as part of my bartending duties.
The point is that most jobs in our industry are a lot of fun and get even more fun when you're really good at it.

People would ask me how long I worked there and I'd say with a genuine smile,
"I don't work here. I just play here until they tell me I have to go home :)."

Why Did I Personally Make the Effort?

I was really scared of being broke and that fueled me to do whatever I had to do so that I could be successful and self-supportive.

The truth is that I started off with nothing. My awesome mom and the GM of our company, Karen Young, raised me by herself since I was five years old. She ROCKS! My dad wasn't in our lives and stopped paying child support. We never owned anything except a beat-up old station wagon.

We lived paycheck to paycheck. It was really tough on my mom and I remember how stressed and scared she was. So when I grew up, I promised myself that I would do whatever it took to be worry-free from having little to no money. I wanted to have freedom from the stresses my mom had faced.

How did I do it?

I failed miserably. Baseball didn't work out because I didn't apply a strong work ethic early enough.

I learned it the hard way. Failure at what I loved. Ouch! It was the best thing that could have happened to me. I decided that I was never going to fail that badly again.

I decided I would really focus on being great at whatever I chose to do and I chose a bartending school. I wanted to make the most amount of money in the shortest amount of time and have fun doing it.

I wanted to be exceptional!

I figured that if I was truly one of the best at whatever I did, then I wouldn't have to worry about finding a good job and keeping it.

It was my survival instinct kicking in. I wanted to be such good all-around bartender, that when I applied for a bartending job, and maybe got a tryout, the bar manager would be thinking,
"Who do I have to let go, to create space for this guy?"
That was my motivation and my plan and it worked too :)

I also wanted to experience all of what the world and this great journey called life had to offer. I quickly learned that I really wanted to learn how to surf and to surf often.

The only problem was that there were no waves within 5 hours of where I lived, so I needed to make more money to pay for travel expenses to get to the places where I could pursue this dream and passion.

So I did. I'm a regular guy who decided early that if I wanted to live a cool life and have freedom from financial worries, I had to make the most of every opportunity. I had to excel. After baseball didn't work out, I chose Bartending.

I put extra special efforts into becoming an <u>extra-ordinary</u> bartender and service giver.

Other than having my car rear ended by a cement truck that was towing a pick-up truck….
That's slowed be down a bit…but got me writing more ☺…

I've lived an incredible life. (See – A Bartender's Life: Living The Dream @ TheBartendingMasters.com)
Why am I telling you all this?
It All happened because I was a bartender. A Service Giver.

All because of the extra efforts I put into being a GREAT service giver and I was way more successful because of it. I'm just a regular guy who tries harder to make the most of what I've got.

If I Can Do It, You Can Do It Too.
- I want to help you become the best bartender that you can be.
- I want you to get the best bartender job.
- I want you to get the best bar shifts.
- I want you to have more fun behind the bar.
- I want you to create a big list of regulars that come just to see you.
- I want you to HUGELY Increase your nightly sales.
And yes, I really want you to make bigger tips and even smaller tips more often!
That's why I created all my training programs…videos, seminars, books, websites and all the other study guides & tests that will soon be available.

So please approach everything you read with an open mind and you will be amazed at how quickly you will start making more tips and having more fun than you already are.

Thanks, Scott Young

P.S. If these books helps you make more money, I suggest that you…

A) Consider becoming an Affiliate Promoter of our store and make 25% - 50% commission from your efforts. Check our website for info and how to sign up.

B) Let us know what you thought.
"If you didn't like our books, videos, websites or our training seminars, please tell us so we can improve.

If you DID like it or us, then please tell us AND everyone you know ☺."
i.e. friends and managers about our websites or Share us on your Facebook wall etc.

Excellence Is An Act Won By
Training And Habituation.

We Are What We Repeatedly Do.

Excellence Then,

Is Not An Act, But A Habit.

- Aristotle

<u>Keep An Open Mind</u>

I have always tried to be very non-combative about the way I teach.

I can't come into your country, your city, your bar and TELL you what's going to work with YOUR customers.

**You are professional,
working service givers,
and experts on your area
and we respect that.**

But what I can do, is tell you about all sorts of things that are working in other bars around the world. It's totally up to you whether you want to try any of them or not.

We, all the people who contributed to this series, really want you to succeed.
This entire series is about giving you ideas on how to be a better All Around service giver.
We're here to help you make more money, for yourself and for your bar.

There are things that suggest that you'll think to yourself….. Yeah….that's not going to work for me ☺.

No problem. We don't expect you to agree with everything we say or write.
Just remember. Everything we've written has come from hard won experience.

Basically, we've screwed up so many times, we've figured out some better ways to do things.
Not perfect, that's too much to expect, but with excellence ☺

So, keep an open mind, be willing to experiment a bit and you may find
that you have more fun and make more money.

"If You Always Do
What You've Always Done,

You'll Get
What You've Always Gotten."
- Anthony Robbins

<u>Make Some Changes And See What Happens</u>

Scott Interviews The Experts. Who Are They?

Hi everyone, I'm Scott and I want to tell you about how these "Expert Interview" sections in this book series came to life.

What experts? Fair question.
Over the course of approx. 2 years, I interviewed well over 200 bartenders, servers, trainers, consultants, managers, owners & brand ambassadors on 11 important topics.

The Team of Experts I've Interviewed have an average of 17 years of experience each.
Some have as many as 30–40 years, so they have all definitely walked the walk.

These people are very passionate about their industry, genuinely want to help make it better and they've done that by telling me/you about their real life stories on important topics.

The interviews are not censored.
They tell you what they really think and what they know and they do it completely.

They share the best lessons of their entire careers and they are super interesting and helpful. I learned a lot from them.

It's like having a top industry professional come to your class and be a guest speaker, except you get a whole bunch of them.

This is like being in the same room with people you would never get a chance to meet and be a "Fly on the Wall" as they talk about their true story successes, failures and their philosophies behind "Why" things happen the way they do.

Our community of seasoned pros offer you knowledge from decades of experience, hundreds of lessons learned, Millions of guests served, and even more drinks poured.

Why limit yourself to learning from one instructor when you can learn from our huge team of experts? That was the concept of this book series.

A few years ago, my car was rear ended by a cement truck that was also towing a pick-up truck. It completely changed my life and almost bankrupted my successful company.

After 2 major surgeries on my spine, and I'd recovered enough to start caring about my company again, I tried really hard to focus on the things that I COULD do and not on my many limitations.
So, I started writing and that's where the "Make Huge Tips" and "Ask The Experts" Series of books, Study Guides and Tests came from.

But as I was writing, I realized that as good as my book was, It was very different from what I had done for 21 years and that was to have interactive discussions with my students and teachers from around the world.

I'm just one guy and I've always conducted our training seminars as an open forum on specific and important topics in order to make the most of our private training time.

We asked everyone in the room for their opinions and stories, their Successes and Spectacular Failures. We all shared, myself included of course and because of this atmosphere, the result was a much more interesting and reality-based learning experience.

So, I came up with the Idea of writing a series of books based on really in depth interviews with some exceptionally successful and experienced bar industry people from around the world that I'd created friendships and/or contacts with.

My recovery was long, still ongoing, but I could write and send e-mails to many people in my network that that I respected and wanted to see what they thought about all sorts of interesting topics.

Here is part of my contact e-mail… Hi, I've been reaching out to many experienced bar people like you to ask if you can please help me out by letting me interview you by my e-mail survey?

It will help create and improve my new e-Book Series (Ask The Bartending Masters).
They are/will be continuing training programs for all levels of bartenders & servers that we've just launched on my brand new site www.TheBartendingMasters.Com

Our Philosophy is This: No one person is the bartending master.

These eBooks are helpful to bartenders & Servers of every level and years of experience.

Just because you've been behind the bar for years doesn't mean that you can't or shouldn't continue learning.

Our guests and our industry are changing and evolving all the time, so we should too.

As you will see below,

I strongly believe that each individual be given full credit, a short bio and a picture next to any comments used as well as a promo of their companies and websites if they had them.

Why?

The purpose of it is to give the reader/student a little background perspective about who each individual person is rather than just a name and some comments who really could be from anyone or completely made up for all you know.

Well, **every one of these people are real bar industry pros**.

Many of them have been friends with me for years and the rest I've made connections with them through Facebook and LinkedIn.

I figured that, you the reader, are already working and successful bar industry people, and will take the suggestions from these other even MORE successful bar industry pro's more seriously when you get to read a little bit about their vast experience as well as see a picture of them.

Part of the greatness of what we're creating is that we're collecting Real advice, life stories etc. from a whole bunch of very successful Bartenders, Managers, Owners and Brand Ambassadors from around the world.

Not just one Scott Young guy writing from his one life experience, etc.

I want you to be able to actually know who these people are, male and female, what kind of bars they work in, how long have they been in the industry etc.

The fact is that great bartenders come in all sorts of shapes, sizes, colours, ages and physical attributes. Our main market is in the US and Canada so most of the people I interviewed are from here but many are from different countries also.

I want you to read them all, in your own time, and have a good think on what they say and then you decide if it makes sense to you.

I don't agree with everything that people said in the interviews, but that's the point.
I wanted to create a diverse cross section of professionals sharing their own REAL stories.
There is always more to learn, even for the most experienced bartenders.

I hope you enjoy reading & learning from these interviews as much as I have.
– Scott

Treat Every Customer

As If They Sign Your Paycheck...

Because They Do. – Unknown

ASK THE EXPERTS: HOW DID YOU GET A BAR JOB?

 Hi everyone,
This part of my interview with you is arguably the most important section of all.

We've all been in this situation. Most of us many, many times and will be again.
I couldn't think of a better way to help people in a big way than to explore this topic with experts like you who have been there, done that and probably seen everything.

I decided to focus on the below subjects and questions.
3 - What Increases The Odds Of A Bartender Getting Hired?
4 - How to Choose Which Bars To Apply At?

Resumes
5 - How to Create a Great Resume?
6 - 5 Things to include
7 - 5 Big Mistakes to avoid
8 - Examples/Stories of Great Resumes?

9 - Examples/Stories of Terrible Resumes

10 - Making a great cover letter?

11 - What were some of the challenges you faced getting a Bartending job?

The Interview

12 - What advice do you have for bartenders?

13 - What was your worst interviewing experience?

14 - What was your best interviewing experience?

15 - What to do/bring/say?

16 - What not to do/bring/say in an interview?

17 - Popular Questions Managers Will ask?

18 - Good Answers?

19 - Good Questions to ask them?

They Hire You. Now What?

20 - 10 Things to do/Ask before your first shift?

21 - Your First Shift. Suggestions on how to do great?

What are The Best Ways to Ask For/Get a Raise, Promotion & Better Shifts?

So, Tell us what you think… Thank you so much for all your help. ☺ Scott Young

I want to Start out with a part of an interview that I absolutely loved.

Remember: This is a collection of interviews.
Feel free to skip around and read what you want to in whatever order you like.

Todd Angman – (I love this guy!! – Scott)
Owner/Operating Partner – Relish The GastroPub & Bar Vancouver, BC, Canada
www.relishthepub.com

Twenty years in the industry. I started in the hospitality industry when I was 14 as a dishwasher at Newlands Golf and Country Club in Langley, then moved to IHOP as a busboy, host (that's right, a male hostess, which was a step up from bussing, so I didn't mind), then eventually made it into the kitchen.

I left there to work in the kitchen for three years, before moving to the front of the house at Earls. That is when my world got rocked and my eyes opened up to the potential of bartending. I served and bartended for a few months before I got promoted to Bar Manager.

Todd Says:
I could be biased on this one, but if you really think that working hard at a job, especially as a bartender, is a crazy effort, you may be in the wrong business.

Go dig some ditches for a while,
then come back and tell me how hard your life was
when you were a bartender!

Bottom line as a bartender,
if you are not having fun at your job,
you are in the wrong line of work.

**Bartending and serving
are some of the most amazing jobs
you can possibly have!**

You get paid to entertain people,
there is usually a lot of booze involved
in the whole serving culture,
and young,
good looking people surround you!

How amazing is that?!!!

What Bar Managers Are Looking For

Les Hemingway Says:
Being in the business 40 years the first thing I look when hiring a bartender is past job experience.

Attendance,
Work record,
How long were they were in their previous positions,
Personality.

And then I call where they worked last and ask bartenders, servers and bar backs who worked with that person.

Calling a manager isn't going to get you anywhere as they cannot voice an opinion by law.

I want a person...
Who is fast,
On time,
Has a great personality,
Smiles,
Can take care of the customers' needs,
Can upsell,
And is willing to help the other staff.

**I don't want
someone who whines,
and
can't work with some of the staff.**

Granted I have staff that doesn't fit all of these examples but I do have staff that isn't going to steal from the club and that too needs to be addressed.

I want someone that is honest and dependable.

These people are hard to find in a country club venue but when you do you pay them well, give them benefits and make sure they stay happy.

Raji Pine
General Manager/Bartender
Always –
The Draft Bar and Grille 34
Harvard Ave,
Allston MA. Instructor/
Performer for
ExtremeBartending.com

I first started as a busser in 1998 at an upscale pool hall/ high volume beer bar. I moved to barback about three months later, started getting trained as a bartender about three months later and started getting bar shifts mixed in with my bar backing shifts for the first year. Since then I have worked at about 10-12 different bars in the Boston area, mostly bars, college bars, neighborhood bars, sports bars high volume bars, clubs, and a few restaurants.

All in the downtown Boston area, some right next to the fabled Fenway Park. In 2002 I was in Las Vegas at Carnival Court and was exposed to flair bartending on a level I had never seen. When I got back I dedicated myself to first finding out how I could learn, and then the ongoing process of learning myself. This led my path to Scott Young and Extreme Bartending and eventually working as an instructor for Extreme Bartending myself.

Raji Says...

I am currently the GM of small bar in Boston called The Draft and in addition I still bartend there five nights a week. It took me a long time to get where I'm at. I worked at some bars which were really great and some which were not. Mostly they were all great some of the time and all made some mistakes some of the time.

I was fortunate that I was able to learn from a number of mistakes I saw bars make over the years so when it came time to teach it to others. I could help them steer in the right direction. I've also had the pleasure of working with some really, really great and knowledgeable people in my time in the bar business, and more importantly been able to pick their brains and have some really great discussions and debates on the best way to make the same drink so to speak.

What Increases The Odds Of A Bartender Getting Hired?

Reputation. Most people I know and jobs I have got have been through word of mouth.

1. I first find out if I know someone working there and ask if they have anything.

Once you've been around for a bit and have built a solid reputation as a bartender and a solid reliable person you can at least get an honest answer. I have had places that weren't looking rearrange things so they could get me in there.

2. If I don't know anybody working there, I'll go hang out there and get to know some of the staff, and I'll let them know I'm a good guy and a solid individual.

I'll let them get to know me a little bit so they have a little more to go on if or when it comes time to make a decision about me. I don't make a fool of myself there or do anything to tarnish their opinion of what I would be like as an employee.

Getting hired has a lot to do with being in the right place at the right time.

Job windows in this business open and close all the time. It's about being there and ready to jump through ON SHORT NOTICE.

Sometimes I'll let people know I'm looking around or ready to make a change and I'll keep popping up so if the right time and place comes up I'm present and in the fore-front of someone's mind.

One of the great things about this business is you don't need an invitation to go see someone or hang out, or an invitation to keep your face fresh in their mind.

I usually make a list of places I'd like to target, If I've never been there I make sure to check it out beforehand.

**All these things increase my odds
because I'm not going in cold,
and in some instances
they are not seeing me for the first time.**

I also keep track of people I've worked with and where they are working and I stay in touch AND SUPPORT them while they are working.

I use them to make more contacts.

This helps support the nights I work, it gets other managers and employees in to see me work (unofficial auditions every night) and helps me create my own network with I can tap into down the road.

Sometimes even years later.

If you are going door to door filling out applications or answering adds, you have done nothing to help yourself get ahead yet.
That is not being proactive.
Once again, if your new to town or have never been there, go there when you're not applying and hang out, meet some staff, relax, casually ask if they hire a lot, who does the hiring, spend a little money, do this a few times.

Keep doing it, they will probably tell you they don't need anyone until they get to know you, the person you talk to may not realize they are looking, also the person you talk to might be trying to protect their own job.

Also try this at a few different places so you have options.

Remember, just because a place is fancy or high priced, doesn't mean the make the most money there.

Look to see what the capacity is?
How much staff do they have on?
Is it busy for the whole time they are open?
Are people actually buying drinks all night or are they just lounging and sipping?

How to Choose Which Bars To Apply At?
How do I choose which bars I apply at? Where ever I can make the most money and have the most fun!

Haha, first off, I have figured out what I would like out of a place that I work at.

I usually look for a balance between money, comfort, stability, atmosphere, location to name some of the few.

First off, I go scout around at potential places to work out and get to know what I can about them.

A) Money, does it look like it's a busy place?

Talk to some people who work there, is it busy all night long?

Most bars in my area are busy for either the first half of the night, or for the late night half of the night.

One of first the things I'll look for is to find one of the few bars that does both, (in my area those are pub style places that serve food, and offer late night bar shenanigans such as dancing and heavy drinking.)

Clubs seem to do only late night business and restaurants do early business.

B) Is the place seasonal?

Will I have to look for work or pick up other shifts when the summer ends?
Is it dependent on a sports team?

If the team does well you are busy, If the team does not will you still be busy, is the team weather dependent, if they make a trade will it have an effect on you?

Personally these are more outside factors I can't control and I would prefer not to be affected by them so I avoid being weather and sports team dependent these days.

C) What is the formula for making money there?

First off, what is the capacity for the place, and how much staff will it take to run it?

Any time you can make 100% of the tips coming in the formula for making money is at its best. The more people it takes to run a busy night the more that % will change.

I've found places that are small enough to do high volume and be run by 2 bartenders and a bar back make for pretty good odds, consistency and a good tip %.

Another thing of note is how a place tips out, does the WHOLE house pool?

Is everybody pulling their weight?
Do all the bartenders pool?
Does each bar pool?
Do they do an hourly for the bartender in times?
Do they just split it?

Try and get an idea what your average take home will be.

D) How many nights are they busy?

I find it rare to find a place with 7 busy nights in a week. Usually 3-4 and few slow ones.

What are they willing to offer you, and will you need to pick a few slow nights to earn your busy shifts?
Do they have day shifts as well?
Is it open all night?
Does it have a full liquor license?

E) How is the place run?

Is there a lot of turn over?
What does the staff say about management?

Do they look like they are having fun at work?
Are the owners around?
Will you even have a relationship with the people you work for?

F) Will you have to pay for parking?

Is it in a safe neighborhood?
What is the crowd like?
Will you be required to jump the bar or do they have a door staff?

These are all a number of things to ask yourself and consider when looking at places.

FYI: You will probably not find a bar which fits all this criteria, and if you do find it… you have only found it. Then you need to get yourself hired at it, haha.

How to Create a Great Resume?
First off, In my experience, I have never been hired from my resume.

I always have one in case someone asked me for one or to drop one off.
(Many places do that just to see if you do have one to see how serious you are)

But you never know. Also if you want to have a good one it will be hard to produce on short notice so having one ready to go is a good thing.

5 Things To Include On Your Resume:

1) Your past work experience that relates to the position you are applying for.

2) Any other work experiences you think might be relevant and might help you.

3) Pictures!
Some places want a head shot, on mine I had a two page collage of pictures of me behind the bar working, pouring shots and entertaining.

When you apply **it's a leap of faith for someone to envision you behind the bar.**

Keep in mind the majority of people applying are embellishing their experiences, and most managers have been fooled a few times in the past and are skeptical of your ability.
If you can help them visualize you behind a bar and your experience you are way ahead of the game. **A picture tells a thousand words.**

4) References:
Include people who know them and can give you a reference.

Now if you've done your homework you hopefully have a connection or two to the place.

Either staff currently there or you might have a mutual friend with the manager, or a mutual acquaintance. (Facebook may be able to help you with this.)

5) **Social Media Page!**
   This is the year 2015 people, it is an age where you can have your own Facebook page as a bartender!

   You can include pictures, VIDEOS, proof you have friends. You can make this online!

**You can walk into a place
with a lap top or iPad
and show this to a manager!**

You can text people links to this!

**You should be building this
your whole career
to make yourself more money
by creating a following!**

And guess what! If you need to change jobs or get an additional job,
YOU ARE ALREADY READY!

BECAUSE OF THIS, SOMEONE MIGHT EVEN APPROACH YOU!!!!

6) Have Videos of You Working!

Have a friend make one, make one yourself!
Once again, it is 2015!
Every phone has a camera and video camera, use it and get creative!

5 Big Mistakes To Avoid

1) Letting your resume become boring!

Keep in mind most resumes…
Go into the trash,
Go into a stack of other resumes,
Only get 10 seconds of attention,
Or get read by the rest of the staff.

It needs to stand out from every other resume on a plain white sheet of paper.

2) Dropping it off and waiting for them to call you.

Make sure to find out who you need to drop it off to and track down that person. Don't be nervous, if your too nervous to approach them, and can't give them a resume with confidence you're not the person they want behind their bar.

3) If your resume is boring and says nothing except what all the other ones I've seen in my lifetime say I will probably not remember it or you.

4) The belief that this is going to be the only thing to get you hired.

We are giving you a lot of information about how to increase your odds of getting hired where you want to work.

Pick and choose but don't rely on any one thing, the resume can be the trap where people create it, put a lot of work into it and drop it off.

They then feel they have 'Applied' and they wait for 'the phone call'.

This is only a small piece in the MIDDLE of this whole process.

5) Having YOUR one resume.

What I mean by that is, a lot of people make a resume, print up 20 copies,
go out and scatter them throughout the world.

Once again, pick and target where you want to work. **Don't be afraid to adjust your resume to the place you are applying to.**
Different places may want to see different sides of you, some places might be turned on to see a more professional side of you whereas some places may want to see you go a little more "coyote ugly." lol

This is the night life business.

Usually it's okay to have some fun with it.
And to show people you CAN have fun.

Making a Great Cover Letter
We want this to be professional, to look good and stand out.
A cover letter does that.

I'm going to assume yours is a couple pages and like a book or a packet.

A good cover letter says open and read me.

Just like a movie billboard sells the movie, or a book cover sells a book.

On mine I had a great picture of me with a big smile complete with title.

Also I had my contact information (not too small)
Make it easy for people to contact you.
If it's hard THEY WON'T DO IT.

What are The Best Ways to Ask For/Get a Raise, Promotion & Better Shifts?
Work hard, offer to take any shift, and take them even if you don't want or need them. Be the person they call first because they know you will say yes and you are reliable.

If you say you want them and you'll take any shift, but then turn down shifts when they offer you are saying you don't really want them.

Offer to come in on your own time for miscellaneous things

Make sure you have done everything in your power to prepare yourself for and window of opportunity, so if it opens you are ready and more than capable of jumping through (and staying through)

Never be a headache, nobody wants a headache, ever.

Face time with the owner or manager or whoever makes the calls or has influence is always good.
Learn how the system works and how you can play it.

Don't limit yourself to just one place.

Always be honest with your bosses, ask if it's okay if you take an additional bar job. Assure them it won't interfere or compete with their interests.

It's always easier to find work while you have a job.

So, network while you have work, make friends and talk to people.
Get to know them and let them know you.

Keep your reputation sacred where ever you are.
Even big cities have small bar scenes.
Everybody knows everybody or knows someone who does.

Ask yourself what you need to do to advance?

Keep in mind nothing has happened until it has, just because you are promised something doesn't mean it's going to happen.

Keep working with a stellar record before and after.

Let people know you are serious.

  **Brian Johnsey** – 24 years in the industry. My career started off in 1990 with a weekend bussing job for a fish buffet in rural Dardanelle, Arkansas. After a few years of bussing tables and washing dishes, I started cooking, catering, ordering and doing basic management while going through high school.

I continued through college and eventually left to join Brinker International (Chili's) to become a regional trainer for Front of the House staff and Bartenders. This turned me on to working with high volume bartenders in the area.

I opened 50+ restaurants in two years before moving to Pensacola, Florida and earning the title of "bartender of the beach" during their summer competitions.
Moving on in my career, my wife and I now own and operate five restaurants in South Carolina that feature 20-35 taps and a full line bar as well.

Brian Says...
What Increases The Odds Of A Bartender Getting Hired?
Typically the bartenders we look for MUST have the personality to keep a guest engaged. Male or Female doesn't matter, and their looks are not key to getting hired.

Its more about being prepared to sell.

If the interviewee can think quickly on their feet to the questions, then it's a pretty good sign they can do so with a guest as well.

Being well rounded in what is going on in the world helps too, so I will typically ask if they have an opinion on a world topic. Since the guests for lunches or dinner might have a need to chat too.

How to Choose Which Bars To Apply At?
Choosing a location to work is just like finding a place to call home.

If you would hang out there that is a good start.

If not, it's going to be like having an apartment with noisy neighbors, you are not going to want to go home.
Thus you will not be successful.

How to Create a Great Resume?
Most of the time the resume plays little to no bearing on whether or not you get hired, but it can restrict you from even getting an interview.

Don't add filler to the resume, simply add the items that have real value to managers. Information on positive reviews from past managers, owners etc..

Everyone says they are the best, hardest worker etc... these are lame.
Keep it...
Simple,
Precise,
Clear,
Unfolded,
On nice paper.

5 Things to include on your Resume
1) Accessible references
2) Dates with month and year
3) Clear job titles (Sandwich artist is for Subway)
4) Have the skills you list, don't lie
5) Keep it to one page.

5 Big Mistakes to avoid
1,2,3,4,5) Don't lie.
Make sure you have great input about each line included in the resume.

Examples/Stories of Terrible Resumes
A bartender applicant said he was formerly the "Communications Manager" for a billion dollar a year company... sold cell phones in the mall.

Making a great cover letter?
Don't fill it with the BS of the hard worker you were or
could be. In three sentences prove why you are a fit for the
company. Make each cover letter specific to the place you
are applying.

**What were some of the challenges you faced getting a
Bartending job?**
Experience is tough to get for high end bars, but show you
are willing to do the grunt work to earn your way.

They key shifts are generally taken, so making sure you
have an availability to cover the slower "off" nights until
you prove yourself.

Suggest bar backing if it's that type of place to prove your
worth.

The Interview
What advice do you have for bartenders?
Show personality, but don't be overly cocky and arrogant.
Too relaxed comes off as aloof and sloppy.

What was your worst interviewing experience?
Boob fell out while talking about wanting to be the best
bartender.

What was your best interviewing experience?
During the interview another guest spilled a drink, he
jumped up and grabbed a towel before any of the other
staff did to assist the guest…. Hired.

What to do/bring/say?
Bring a copy of the resume, drink menus you may have created that are still in use, training materials that you use, have a pen, bar key, and wine opener….

What if you get hired on the spot?
Are you really ready?

What not to do/bring/say in an interview?
Cell phone.

Popular Questions Managers Will ask?
Why are you here today?
i.e. why if you are so good are you unemployed or looking for a job.

Good Answers?
"I'm looking for a place that better suits what I have to offer or what I want to learn about."

Good Questions to ask them?
Why are you looking for bartenders given that everyone seems to want to be one.

They Hire You. Now What?

10 Things to do/Ask before your first shift?
Learn the dish washer's name.

Learn about the quirks of policies
Ie. smoke breaks, dinner options,
who covers if you have to go to the bathroom,
how do tabs work,
who all is going to get to my cash drawer.

Your First Shift. Suggestions on how to do great?
Be calm and win ONE guest at a time.

What are The Best Ways to Ask For/Get a Raise, Promotion & Better Shifts?
Keep a log of your Sales for the shifts that you operate.

Make sure that you are increasing the sales and efficiency on your shifts.
Show your worth.

Make sure you availability matches to what the needs are, don't have too many requests off for at least a month prior to your request.

Ask a few questions,
"what are things you feel I can do better to earn my way into the _____ shift?" "what do you feel makes _____(employee) better fit for _____ shift.

Jeff Reid – I have over 25 years of experience in hospitality, management, ownership and operations, and have had the good fortune to work for organizations that are the very best at what they do, and with people that are exceptional in the industry.

In my career, so far I have trained a workforce in excess of 500 people, and have been responsible for sales in excess of 75 million dollars, and served an incredible number of customers over the years.

I have also worked as a bartender with/beside Scott Young at the Roxy for many years as well as his manager, mentor, religious counsellor, fashion advisor and dog walker, and all around smart-ass friend.

Jeff Says:
What Increases The Odds Of A Bartender Getting Hired?
A genuine interest in the venue and knowledge about who they are and how they operate. Do your homework!

How to Choose Which Bars To Apply At?
Volume is an easy way, but don't underestimate smaller, less popular venues.

Look to place where you can do high overall sales, either though small guest checks with a large volume of people, or a large guest check through a small volume of people.

Also look for venues with happy staff, and low staff turnover. Make sure it is more than just money that attracts you.

Resumes

5 Big Mistakes to avoid

1. Spelling and grammar errors

2. Overstating simple things.

If you last job was dishwasher, say dishwasher. Not glassware sanitation manager.

3. Keep it short.
Only relevant information.

I am only going to spend 30 seconds reading your resume. What do you what me to know?

4. Make sure your contact information is correct, and make sure I can contact you.

If you don't have voicemail and I can't leave you a message, how am I going to contact you to cover a shift once I hire you?

If I can't reach you or leave a message, I will move on to another candidate.

5. Crumpled or folded resumes.
Give me something in good condition.

What were some of the challenges you faced getting a Bartending job?
None. I am awesome.
Scott Says: He really is a smart ass, but he's also correct.

The Interview
What advice do you have for bartenders?
Be prepared, and ask relevant questions. You should be interviewing me too.

What to do/bring/say?
Copy of your resume, references, **questions you have to ask me written out**

Your First Shift. Suggestions on how to do great?
Learn how the venue operates before you give advice on what they should change.

What are The Best Ways to Ask For/Get a Raise, Promotion & Better Shifts?

How often to ask?
Annually

What increases your odds?

If you have a valid argument for an increase in pay other than just being there for a year.

Are you making more money for the business?

Are you saving them money?

How are you worth more than a year ago?

How are you more valuable than the next person who wants your job?

How do you bring it up?

Be up front. Ask if you can have a performance review.

Get information from your boss on his or her version of your performance before you ask for a raise. Make sure you both agree on how well you are doing your job.

Gary Muise

I started doing security while attending Acadia University and soon realized that on the floor and behind the wood was the place to be......after doing that for a few years I went to work a new bar & grill that was opening as a bartender....within three months I was promoted to Bar Manager which I stayed at for a little of a year. I then moved to Halifax to work at one of the busiest student bars JJ Rossy's.....I stayed with JJ's for 11 years being promoted to the General Manager of three operations.

Then about 10 years ago I was brought on board at Grafton Connor as part of some succession planning and now I'm the VP of Operations of 20 operations with over 550 employees.

Gary Says:
What Increases The Odds Of A Bartender Getting Hired?
Personality……I can train anyone to serve and be a bartender….
I can't train you to have the right personality …
That's your parents' problem.

How to Choose Which Bars To Apply At?
Find a bar that fits you…….if you like dance music work at a dance bar,
you like sports work at sports bar……..
life to too short to work somewhere that you don't enjoy.
How to Create a Great Resume?
No more than two pages, no color, keep the format clean and for the love of god use SPELL CHECK.

White paper with black ink and a full color picture (head shot) is the perfect resume for me. Colored paper to me is too cheesy.

5 Things to include
#1 – Current address (I hire people who live close by).

#2 – Phone number with voice mail….I only call once

#3 – One sentence that will make you stand out

#4 – References (industry related)….your little baseball coach means nothing to me

#5 – A picture……this is the hospitality business and people want to be served by good looking people

5 Big Mistakes to avoid

#1 – Spelling mistakes,

#2 – Addressing the cover letter to the wrong business,

#3 – Wrong address and/or phone number

#4 – Weird resume formats (on average I look at a resume for 1 min…..

If it's too hard to figure it gets put to the side

#5 – A resume that was designed for another profession.

Examples/Stories of great Resumes?
Way too many but the good ones all good offered jobs

Examples/Stories of Terrible Resumes
Way too many but they all ended up in the can

Making a great cover letter?
Sell yourself

The Interview –
What advice do you have for bartenders?
Show up 15 minutes early,
Have a copy of your resume (references if not included),
Dress professional
And don't be a smoker (I don't hire smokers…..cost me too much wasted time)

Get to the person who does the hiring......just don't leave it with the bartender.

What was your worst interviewing experience?
Too many to explain.....one person showed up late for three interviews.....
needless to say they didn't get offered a position.

What was your best interviewing experience?
I have hired people who started on the spot (so you better be ready to go)

What to do/bring/say?
Resume, references, SIN, banking info.....show them you are ready to work

What not to do/bring/say in an interview?
Don't be an idiot

Popular Questions Managers Will ask?
What are your strengths and weaknesses?
What makes you a good bartender?
Why should I hire you?

Good Answers?
What are your Strengths---
I like people,
I am available all the time,
I won't cause you any headaches.

What makes me a good bartender?.....
I can talk to anyone.....

I am always prepared for the busiest of nights….
the customer in front of me is the most important person
in my world for that 30 seconds.

Why you should hire me?……
I will make you lots of money and make your
customers feel special.

Good Questions to ask them?
Who will be my direct report be?
Who will be training me?
When do I start?

They Hire You. Now What?

10 Things to do/Ask before your first shift?
(in no order)

#1 – Who stocks the bar?

#2 – Where is the ice machine

#3 – What are the prices?

#4 – What do I wear?

#5 – Do I bring my own float?

#6 – Do I bring my own bar tools

#7 – Who am in working with?

Your First Shift.
Suggestions on how to do great?
Stay positive and ask lots of questions.

What are The Best Ways to Ask For/Get a Raise,
Promotion & Better Shifts?

When to ask?
After you just killed a shift and sold a lot.

What to ask?
Be to the point......raises rarely happen.....better shifts is
the way to go

What increases your odds?
Be the highest performer

How do you bring it up?
Ask to speak in private on an off day when the boss isn't
busy

 **Jim Brown**
I have close to 30 years' experience in Food
and Beverage, from Nightclub Bartender
in the busiest nightclubs in Calgary to
Executive Director of Food and beverage
with major hotel chains.

I have worked as a General Manager for major restaurant
chains to owning my own bar. I have consulted for several
nightclubs across Western Canada.

Jim Says:
What Increases The Odds Of A Bartender Getting Hired?
This is a very easy answer

1. <u>Personality</u>, <u>Personality</u>, <u>Personality</u>.
I can teach anyone to be a good bartender and make great tasting drinks,
but I can't train a personality into a bartender.

In 30 years in this business the bartenders who get hired and make the most money have a great personality, they can interact with the guests and they develop a following which makes the bar money.

2. Be honest on your resume.
The bar community in most cities everyone knows everyone.
If you are lying on your resume, we will find out.

3. Dress to impress.
Don't come to interview dressed like you just crawled out of bed.

How to Choose Which Bars To Apply At?
When I started in the bar business, I took a job as a service bartender at a very busy restaurant. I worked at the job for over a year, during that time I learned some quintessential bartending skills, Speed, Drink Recipes, Bar cleanliness and how to pour and interact.

During my time there I started hanging out with other bartenders who worked in the big nightclubs. I learnt which bars were the better bars to work for.

One of the bartenders I hung out with mentioned they needed a bar porter at their club and that he would put in a good word for me.

I got the job, I busted my ass for three months then I got my chance, a bartender called in sick. Within a month I got into the bartender rotation.
The point I'm trying to make is…

Make the most out of chances and opportunities that you are given.

Do your homework, work hard and have a great attitude.

Todd Angman – 20 years in the industry Owner/ Operating Partner – Relish The GastroPub & Bar Vancouver, BC, Canada www.relishthepub.com

Continued from above…
I got a job bartending at a nightclub in Abbotsford called Animals.

I did that for a few years before the travel bug grabbed me and I left to spend 6 ½ months in New Zealand, Australia, and Fiji, which was one of the best times in my life!!

I worked at The Cat's Meow on Granville Island, where after a month or so, I took over as Bar Manager. It was a great little place that wasn't corporately run, my first taste of what ownership would be like. I worked at the Meow for a year before I was off again. This time, it was Calgary, where I was part of the opening team for a new nightclub called Tequila. The summer was great in Calgary, but then the winter came!
I am not made for cold weather; so back to Vancouver I came.

Not much after moving back, four friends and I started working on a business plan to open up our own place. And hence, Relish the Restaurant and Lounge was created!
For 5 years, Relish was a 250-300 seat restaurant and lounge.

It is amazing the amount of mistakes that you can make on your first venture, but as long as you learn from them and can keep yourself afloat, it's a great experience!

After five years, we downsized to an 85-seat pub, which has been amazing for now almost four years, and hopefully will continue to be for the next 25 years!!!

Todd Says:
What Increases The Odds Of A Bartender Getting Hired?

I think you have to pick the places that you want to apply to carefully and then go for it. I, along with many others, don't necessarily have the "Chachi look" that a lot of nightclub owners/managers are looking for.

Not to say that you can't get hired at the popular clubs, but you will have to work harder than some of the other applicants.

For most new bartenders,
I would definitely choose a restaurant to start.

It is easier, better training, and your chances are far better of getting hired.

If you are lucky enough to get hired into a busy nightclub and don't know what you are doing, you won't last long.

Before going into apply, be ready for anything.
Always bring a few pens to fill out an application.

Nothing is worse than someone coming in to apply for a job then asking to borrow a pen. STRIKE ONE already!

Don't be afraid to dress nice and shave, like you actually care, and be prepared to answer questions about the bar.

Yes, this means you may have to visit the bar/restaurant before you actually apply.

Be fast on your toes in answering, but don't get caught in a lie.

> Manager: "Have you ever been here before?"
> You: "Yes, absolutely!"
> Manager: "What is your favourite menu item?"
> You: "UMMMMMMMM?"

You just got caught in a lie, and they know it.
You are also more nervous than you were going into the interview.

Be yourself and try to relax and have fun in the interview. Confidence is great, but don't be over cocky.

How to Create a Great Resume?
Make sure your resume is well laid out on the page, organized and clear.

Spend the extra money at Staples or home to use the good paper and try and stand out from everyone else.

Things to include
A few good references. Please leave off the bad ones (you would be surprised)

Big Mistakes to avoid
A few mistakes to avoid may seem small, but add up. Spelling mistakes, illegible writing, bad references, made up references, or other lies that you may get caught in, are generally things that should be avoided.

Examples/Stories of great Resumes?
When I'm interviewing, I don't really spend a lot of time reading the resume to be honest. I like to talk to the person and get a feel for whom they really are.

I read the resume to see where they worked and to see if I know any of the references, but good resumes don't really stand out.

It's the bad ones that do.

Examples/Stories of Terrible Resumes
I have had a few hand written resumes handed to me, which I wonder if this is a joke,
or is this person serious.

If you don't have a computer, go to the library and type it out.

Spelling mistakes and grammar are no excuse with spell check today, and the bartending world being so small; don't say you have worked somewhere you haven't. We will find out.

I had a roommate once that pretty much guaranteed me a job at the restaurant that he worked at. I printed a crappy resume out on his computer and went in over confident and didn't even get a second of the mangers time. Had I spent 10 minutes properly crafting my resume, it could have been a totally different story.

Making a great cover letter?
Cover letters are great, but I think they only make an impact if you are mailing in your reference.

My dad once got a resume mailed in a shoebox with a shoe with the cover letter saying, "Now that I have my foot in the door, let me introduce myself…"

That letter may not have gotten them hired, but it did make them stand out.

What were some of the challenges you faced getting a Bartending job
I have always looked young which at 37; I love now, but destroyed my chances at many bar jobs.

A few of the bars that I applied at, I convinced the manager to let me work a shift for free. I proved to them that I was the best person for the job, and was hired!

What was your worst interviewing experience?
I have had many! There have been a few that I was just too nervous and shy to even look them in the eyes when answering questions.

If you don't have the confidence, fake it! I realize from my past that it is not always that easy, but try.

The Interview
What advice do you have for bartenders?
Let me see your fun personality during the interview!
I know we can all be nervous, but try and have fun with it.

If you are fun during your interview, chances are you will be fun while you work!

As my dad once told me,
it is always good to have a firm handshake
and
look people in the eye when you meet someone,
especially
if you are looking to get hired.
It shows confidence.

Try and be yourself, but the best "yourself" you can.

I try and ask questions about your hobbies, books read, what you do in your spare time.

Not that I really care, but I'm trying to get you to relax and be yourself.

And to see how you react to a question that you weren't expecting.

What was your best interviewing experience?
My best interview was one that I didn't even know was an interview!
I was in Australia at 4:00 AM on New Year's Day.
My friends had all gone back to the hostel, but I still had a full drink, so I stayed and chatted with the regulars at the bar.

As 6:00 AM rolled around, the guy next to me told me he was the GM of the bar and offered me a job!

What not to do/bring/say in an interview?
To this day, I still don't think this was a bad question on my part, but I was having a fantastic interview, and I asked what the restaurant did in sales on an average week.

I know that in most restaurants the sales are around 30-40% food and 60-70% booze,
so I wanted to gauge in my head how busy the bar was.

With one question, I lost the job.
The interview ended abruptly, and I was leaving the building shocked.

I didn't think it was too personal, but apparently he did, so maybe leave that one until after you get hired!

Popular Questions Managers Will ask?
As I said, I like to ask questions that have nothing to do with the job, just to see how different people react and if they are quick enough to adapt.

One of my least favourite questions that I have been asked is,
"What is your biggest weakness?"
because if you are not prepared for it, you will stumble on it.

I have also been asked,

"Tell me about a time when you made a mistake, and what you did to correct it".

Again, the manager doesn't really care about the answer, but how you react to the question.

Answers?
The good answers to me are the funny ones or the ones that people answer right away with confidence.

It is not as important what you say
to some of these questions,
but
how you answer them.

If you need a quick second to think of something, **stall with, "That is a great question!!"**
It will give you a second or two to collect your thoughts without seeming like you don't know the answer.

Good Questions to ask them?
How many hours are they looking for a week, i.e. full time or part time. What you will be doing if you get hired.

They Hire You. Now What?
Once you are hired, it's ok to show initiative.
But don't try and change the world right away.

You need to fit in and get along with the rest of your bar team, or you may not last.

It may not be fair, but I've seen it a few times, where the new guy comes in and tries to change everything to make it "better", which it honestly could be.

But right away the rest of the team has the attitude of "Who is this new guy, coming in here trying to change us?"

Get to know the others and make small suggestions, to make it less dramatic, but work your butt off from day one.

Lead by example, and most people will eventually follow your lead.

What are The Best Ways to Ask For/Get a Raise, Promotion & Better Shifts?

For me, I've never really asked for a raise.

I have asked to be Bar Manager, which came with a raise, but also a lot more work.

The only advice I would give on this would be to not just ask for a raise, but ask, "What else can I do to make some more money?"

A small distinction, but you are offering something more to your boss than just what you have already been doing.

Kevin Reuter – I have over 15 years' experience behind the bar that includes having served about every type of clientele there is.

I have also had the pleasure of serving President and Mrs. Barbara Bush. But I have always loved to work in a place with a fast pace, loud music, and people having a good time.

Kevin Says...
Increase your odds of getting hired
First and foremost, and I have found this out after moving to a small city from one with 5 million people in it, dress according to the type of bar you are applying at.

Or, you could say according to where you live AND the type of bar.

For the most part, I would always suggest, at the very least, a button down shirt and tie with slacks.

However, if you're applying at a small bar in a small city or town, you may want to try nice jeans and a collared shirt.

I've even gone into some places, after realizing I was over-dressing at times, wearing jeans, a cool T-shirt, baseball cap, and clean tennis shoes.

As long as you look nice in what you choose to wear and the look fits YOU.

Sports bars are perfect for wearing what I just described, as are smaller bars that one bartender does everything in.

Always, always, always bring two pens in with you.
Even if you are just dropping of a resume. You never know when an owner will ask you to fill out an application because they are looking at that moment.

And believe me when I say, they WILL ask you if you need a pen, and it is strike one if you do not. The 2nd one, obviously, is in case one doesn't work for some reason.

How to Choose Which Bars To Apply At?
Another good practice is to go to a prospective place as a customer and just hang out for an hour or so.

But use this time to, unassumingly, watch how the flow of things is there.

Look for things that go wrong and why they did.
If you can work a comment in during an interview that relates to a possible issue they're having, you probably just got hired.

But, don't say something like, 'I noticed the other day in here…..'
Work it to where you ask it as a question on how they do things, or IF they do something a certain way.

In other words, have a solution to their issue or don't bring it up.

Scouting places before applying can supply you with all sorts of information that will only make you look better in an interview.

For example, see what system they use and if it's one you have used before you can use it in an interview. Like, 'Do you use Aloha behind the bars? Oh, good because I'm already very familiar with that system.'

Even if it's just about any other touch screen system, they're all basically similar to use.

Scouting also allows you to see what managers and owners are wearing.

If they are wearing T-shirts and tennis shoes, then it's a safe bet you don't need to wear a tie when you go in.

However, for an interview, I suggest wearing shirt, tie, slacks, and dress shoes no matter what type of bar it is.

The type of bar you should be looking for is one where you are comfortable knowing you have the skills and knowledge to jump in and go once hired.

If, like many of us, you learn fast and aren't uncomfortable going into a place that, for example, does five times the volume than you've ever done, I say go anywhere you want.

I did and when I was hired at places where my experience and skill level didn't quite meet their standards, I faked it 'til I made it. I also feel this is the best way to learn.

But, only do it if you are confident about it and you also don't mind asking questions that you may think make you look ignorant.

And NEVER ask a manager or owner a bar question, only other BT's.
Chances are management won't know the answer anyway, and you WILL look ignorant. And find a BT or two who don't think they're an all-star to ask anything you don't know.
Asking the wrong person the wrong question could result in the whole bar hearing about it two seconds after you ask it.

A bit more on choosing the right bar for you.
If I had to choose one word to describe how you should feel about any bar you see as a prospect for work, it would be 'confidence'.

If you feel uneasy or overwhelmed by a place, forget it and move on.
You have to feel confident for so many reasons, especially those just starting out.

As your experience grows so will your confidence in being able to work anywhere you want. Not to mention, a lack of confidence will show through as soon as you walk in the door. And, will come through in the way you converse with mgmt., hiring and other.

So, if the only experience you have is from a school for bartending, but you have confidence in the skills you have and that you can easily pick up the skills you don't, then go for it.

Resumes

This has never been one of my strongest suits, mostly because I suck at formatting anything. I do have some advice, though.

I suggest either using the Templates provided in Outlook or find them on the web. That's to begin with.

5 things you want to include – When I'm looking for a bar job...

1. I make a resume that has ONLY past and present bar jobs and experience at each.

2. Tell them any special responsibilities you had.
   Some that fit this category are having done liquor inventories, were in charge of X amount of bar-backs, scheduling, helped with ideas for special events.

3. Always include three references and try to use people who you have worked for, and or, know who are high up in what they do, such as owners of companies etc..

   If you happen to be acquainted with a big name in the city you live, use them as a reference. But always be sure to let those people know that you have put them as a reference for a job you are seeking.

4. I suggest not to get too wordy on a bar resume.

Make it short as far as describing duties and such.

Honestly, most bar jobs I've ever interviewed for, they have been more interested in my verbal skills during the interview and if it is evident that I know what I'm talking about.

I have been asked less than five times about a past job that is on my resume.

5. For those going for their first bar job, I say get a little creative with your resume and let them know how your skill sets, no matter where you got them, will relate into the bar world.

But, never lie or exaggerate your skills or knowledge because if you are hired they will find that out soon enough.

There's no need to do that anyway if you have what is needed to be a good, or great, bartender you will be able to mold your resume, using the experience you do have, to fit the job desired.

The Interview and how to get them quicker and more often, and get hired when you do.
Obviously, you will get more interviews as your experience grows and there are ways in which to make that happen quicker.

When I moved from a city of 25,000 about 30 minutes south of Houston, TX to the city of Houston with a population of 5 million plus, let's just say that the experience I had gained to that point wasn't going to get me a job at a gentlemen's club.

So, what I did was go to the top 10 catering companies in Houston to apply.

I ended up getting hired by one that did wedding receptions out of a real nice building in the heart of the city.

I was there for three years and by the time I left I had tons of experience in high volume, fast paced bartending.

I was also an event supervisor for the bars for over a year there, which is great on a resume.

That led to me being hired at another catering company that was always in the top 3 in Houston and # 1 twice in the six years I was with them.

Now, you may be thinking, 'catering…who wants to bartend for a catering company? Where's the fun in that?'

Well, weddings with an open bar are an absolute blast to work and the tips flow like water. Not to mention, catering companies in bigger cities pay good hourly rates as well.

And, you will learn more about the do's and don'ts to great service than anywhere else. At least I did.

If that's not enough, you will gain experience in all sorts of settings;
which include fast-paced, even-paced, to a slow but elite style of service from behind the bar.

I worked for several of them at once and the lowest rate I was hired at was $14/hr, and that quickly went up.

If you're good, or if you work to be good, you will be rewarded for it.

So, you may have to start out doing something different than your ultimate goal but, if you are passionate about tending bar, I assure you that you will enjoy just about anywhere you land a job.

The important thing is to get the experience where you can and as fast as you can.

When I had finally had enough of that type of bartending, I had amassed about eight years of experience, and could just about get hired anywhere after that, and did.

The Interview
Now, once you begin to get more interviews you will notice that there are certain things you should always do and say, and that the types of interviews and interviewers will vary as much as the types of bars out there do.

Here is my list of definite do's and don'ts in an interview.

Never, ever do these things.

1. Chew gum

2. Interrupt the interviewer

3. Slouch or have bad posture or body language

4. NEVER bad talk ANY other bar or place you have worked

5. Fidget or move around.

6. Lie about anything. (It will cost you at some point in a very bad way)

7. Ask for an unreasonable starting wage.

   It is better in our industry to say something like, 'Well, I'm really not very familiar with how you decide wages. Maybe you can give me an idea how it works here?'

8. Don't be arrogant, but do be confident.

   And not being sure of a question and saying so is more a show of confidence than a lack of it.

These are things you always want to do.

1. **Make eye contact with the interviewer when answering or being asked a question.**

   In moments of no one speaking, it's okay and even good to look around a little. Staring at the interviewer the entire time is not good and can be very intimidating to people.

2. **Bring two pens and I always bring two copies of my resume**.

   There is a good reason for this.

   The interviewer may not be able to find the resume you already dropped off.
   If so, you have one to give them.

   The second one is for filling out your application.
   That way you can refer to it for the dates and places you have worked, as well as your reference's information.

   Makes filling an application out much faster.

3. **Sit up straight.**

   It's always best to begin the interview by sitting up straight with your feet flat on the floor, and hands resting on your legs.

   Depending on the sense of formality the interview takes on, or if you see the interviewer relaxing towards you, it's okay to cross one leg over the other.

   But, not in the way that crossed leg will have your knee protruding out.
   In simple terms, more like a female than a male would normally do it.

4. **Speak clearly and not loudly, but not softly either.**

5. **Make your answers as concise as possible.**
   If you find yourself rambling on, just cut it off and excuse yourself for doing so.

6. **Let your passion for bartending show.**
   But let them know you are willing to do whatever they need to start.

   Restaurants, Sports Bars, and Catering Companies normally hire bartenders from the staff that has worked for them a while already.

   However, I am living proof that you can walk into any of these places and get hired as a BT. I've done it around 10 different times and it will be your experience that makes the difference.

7. **Always research any place before the interview.**
   Learn the history they have, read their mission statement, what they serve if they do food, and use this to ask questions about or just to compliment them on.

Perhaps the best advice I could give on interviews is to be ready for anything.

Most interviews will go about the same, but you are sure to run into someone who has their own special idea about how one should be run.

I've been in some where **they will test your ability to adapt quickly and problem solve**, and the methods used can be quite creative.

If this happens, most importantly, do not panic.
Some interviewers will do all sorts of things to catch you off guard to see how you will react. And that is mostly what these types of people are looking for.
How you react to an unexpected circumstance.
Even if you are at a complete loss by something, just take a quiet deep breath, stay calm, and do the best you can on whatever exercise they put you through.

If you panic or let your mind race with possible solutions to their question, you have just failed the test.

Even if you don't come up with what they are looking for, as long as you remain calm and get creative, you will pass their test in most cases.

So, any interview you go to, go into it with your mind completely open to any possibilities as far as what you may be asked, or asked to do.

This will help immensely with how you initially react to some crazy question.

I interviewed at an apartment complex once for a job showing apartments.
The girl who interviewed me, literally, read off of a list of three pages of questions.

And there wasn't a "normal" question on the list.

I couldn't believe it at the time. But, I stayed calm and confident and I think I did a good job. Although, I didn't get the job. And this brings me to a touchy issue that can arise in any interview.

One question you are almost assured to be asked in any interview is,
'Where do you see yourself in 5 years?'

This is where it is important to know the position the interviewer holds and to be able to gauge how they feel about you.

And I know this is not easy and not always possible. But, it is possible that the interviewer can turn out to be intimidated by you, your knowledge and experience, and the answers you give to the point where they end up worried you will take their job.

Even if their job is the last job on earth you would ever want! Unfortunately, there isn't a whole lot you can do about this one.

But it is a good reason for you to make sure you are humble during the process, and not arrogant or overly confident.

It is a tough road to navigate, and you will only get better with it by the more interviews you go through. Which is a great example of how vital the information in these pages can be for you.

Knowledge is power and don't ever think it isn't.
So, I suggest soaking up as much of the knowledge found here as you can.

It will only serve to enhance the power and control you will have at your disposal as you move through your career. And that goes for any career choice you make.

Erin Ferreira I have been in the restaurant and bar industry for 14 years. I have held job titles from bartender to general manager. I currently work on the Las Vegas strip as a flair bartender for the Margaritaville Casino.

Scott Says:
Erin is one of the best female flair bartenders I've ever seen and is in my top all around 10 bartenders I've ever met. Male or female.
She also came in 4th place overall in the Pro-division against all the big boys at The Legends Of Bartending World Championship.

Erin Says...
What Increases The Odds Of A Bartender Getting Hired?
The obvious answer is to go into the interview looking and feeling great.

This means not hung over, not hungry, not sick, and functioning with all cylinders at 100%.
Wear business casual clothing, look presentable.

Also, pay attention to the **3 Hs**:
Hair, **H**ands, and **H**eels.

Remember, you are selling yourself.
You want to look your best to feel your best.
This is the basic "let's get hired" approach.

How can we go even further to increase the odds of getting the job?

Different bars are looking for different kinds of bartenders.

A bartender will increase his or her odds of being hired by researching the bar where they are applying. When going into the interview with an understanding of the company and its goals, the bartender just increased his or her chances of being hired.

For example, if you apply for a sports bar whose team is the New England Patriots, then go in knowing a few stats for that team.

If the bar is a mixology bar focusing on cocktails with fresh and innovative ingredients, then study their drink menu and become familiar with the products they use.

Most businesses have a website or a Facebook page where an applicant can find out all kinds of information about the business without getting off of their butt!

Why not learn as much as you can and find the aspect of the company you admire, relate to, or strive to be like.

Why do you want the job?
They may ask you this question.

Instead of answering,
"Because I have bills to pay."

Why not answer,
"Because I also share a passion for mixology and the New England Patriots. I admire that this company gives back to the community through charity. I think I can learn and grow as a bartender in this company."

The great part is that you can sell yourself using specifics instead of generalizing.

How to Choose Which Bars To Apply At?
Not all bars are created equal. Just as each bar is looking for different kinds of bartenders, we bartenders have to know which kind of bars fit our needs.

I once had a bartending job that lasted five hours.
I'm not sure why I even stayed that long.

I've also had a bartending job that lasted five years.
The difference between the two?
I was proud to work at one and ashamed to work at the other.

Again, research is the key to figuring out if a bar that is hiring is a place where you will be happy working. Granted, you may have to kiss a few frogs to find the prince, but diligence is key to ending up at a bar where you are happy and can thrive as a bartender.
If I had done a little research before taking the job at "yucky" bar then I would never have accepted the position. A little recon would have alerted me to the fact that this bar was losing money and undertook some questionable tactics in order to save some dough.

Personally, I look for a bar with a good reputation.

I talk to current employees.
I look the bar up online.
I check out their clientele.
I check to see if the bar is clean and organized.

Basically, I put the bar through an interview before I have my interview.

Never again do I want to waste my time or the manager's time if I know I do not want to work there.

They Hire You. Now What?
10 Things to do/Ask before your first shift?

1. **Make sure you have all the tools you need to do your job.**

   Does the bar provide everything you need?

   In my bar bag for work I have:
   - Pens
   - Wine opener
   - Bottle opener
   - Lighter .
   - POS card, employee card, *TAM card, *Health card, *Sheriffs card

                              (*Las Vegas requirements)

   - Whistle
   - Business cards

   For a previous job I would also bring my own mixing tins, bar spoon, and muddler.

2. **Make sure you know where emergency equipment is.**

   Fire extinguisher, emergency exits, eye wash, first-aid kits, and any emergency procedures.

3. **Make sure you have proper footwear.**

   Most bars like slip-resistant shoes for all employees.

Your shoes

are the

most important part of your uniform.

Happy feet = happy bartender.

4. **Ask what the standard pour is at the bar.**

   Some bars pour 1.25 ounce for a standard drink, some pour more or less.

5. **Familiarize yourself with the drink menu before your first day.**

   This will save time during training. If they have one, ask the manager for a drink menu that includes exact ounces for each of the drinks on the menu.

6. **Have the proper attire before you start.**

   They may provide uniforms, or they may just tell you to wear a certain kind of shirt/pants.

   Just make sure you are ready to go with the correct uniform on your first day.

7. **If you have the opportunity to sit at the bar where you are about to start working, Do it!**

   Hang out and get a feel for the place.

I do not recommend drinking at the place where you work or are about to start working.

Order a non-alcoholic beverage and just observe the bartenders and guests interact.

8. **Get a good night sleep the night before.**

   Be well rested so you can take in all the information that is about to come your way! Take notes if you need to.

9. **Get familiar with the brands that the bar uses before you start.**

   Especially if this is your first bartending job.
   There may be some brands you have never heard of!

10. **Go into work with a good meal in your belly so you have fuel for your body and mind. :)**

 **Martin Duffy** – I have nearly 25 years in the industry.
I worked as a bartender for 12 years (4am bars, Med Taverna, Jazz Clubs & hotel Bars) until going full-time as the Diageo Master of Whisky in Chicago from 2003 to 2011, with a 2 year stint as the Diageo Ireland Reserve Brand Ambassador.

For the past year I have been working at the Benedictine National Brand Ambassador. With a few years working freelance for such companies as Brown-Forman, LVMH,

Campari, Redemption Rye, InterBevUSA and starting out as a server.

Please let me know if I can be of any future assistance.

Martin Says...
What Increases The Odds Of A Bartender Getting Hired?

When going in for an interview for any job, **the 3Ps** always come in handy -
> **P**ersonality
> **P**romptness
> **P**rofessionalism.

Prompt
Keeping a prospective boss waiting to interview you for a job because you are running late will just give them time to start thinking that you really don't want this job that badly, and that they have better things to do than wait for you.

This is not the mood you want them in when you sit down for the actual interview.

Personality
Let your sparkling self shine through!

Be sure to get plenty of rest the night before and have a good breakfast, so that when you arrive for the interview who have vim and vigor.

You want your prospective boss to see the guy that will woo customers to his bar.
Smile, ask questions, be courteous and refrain from critiquing anything about the bar.

Always be positive, and let a little humor show as well.

Professionalism
Always be prepared.

Have a couple copies of a nicely typed resume.
Visit the bar a few times and study how the other employees dress, the style of their performance and the level of the clientele (hipster, oldsters, yuppie, etc.).

Look sharp, but dress in the manner of the bar itself.
If it is a high end bar, wear a suit coat (a tie isn't necessary).

Know your cocktails,
but better yet,
know
your spirits.

Cocktails can go by many different names, but spirit categories and brands always have the same name.
Study them!

How to Choose Which Bars To Apply At?
Simple....go to them.

Visit a prospective bar/restaurant/pub during normal working hours and ask yourself the following questions:

- Are the current employees the type of people that you would want to work?

- Is the clientele people you would want to deal with eight hours a day?

- Do they make the sort of drinks that you would be comfortable making?

- Is the bar too high end or too low end for you?

- Are the bar's prices too high for what they are serving?

- Engage with the staff and after a while find out if they are happy with the amount of tips they receive.
- Have they been working at the bar for many years?
  If you think that they are a good server/bartender, then this is always a very good sign.

- Are the drinks/food of good quality?

- What type of spirit/beer selection do they have?
  Do they have a number of high end spirits and do people seem to be drinking them?

- Actually stepping into a bar during normal working hours is the only way to know for sure what the environment like will be like when you will be working there.

How to Create a Great Resume?
Put only the major important items in the resume.

If you did something truly fantastic once, leave that for the cover letter or save it for the interview.

Employers do not want to read novels, they just want to have an idea of whether you can do the job or not.

5 Things to include
- Contact info (Name, address, phone, e-mail)
- Objective – what is it that you want out of getting this job.
- Last five bars that you worked at
- The position that you worked at these jobs
- Additional experiences/certifications that would apply to working at a bar (beer cicerone, sommelier, bar courses, cocktail awards/competitions, etc.)

5 Big Mistakes to Avoid

- Don't mention that you just graduated from bartending school.
  It is the kiss of death.

  You can say that you continuously attend bar courses and seminars.

- Never reject a job because you are not getting the prime shifts.

Take what you are given and work your way up to the best nights behind the bar.
Earn that right!

- Never expect the bar to just call you back
  – call them after a few days and check on the status of your consideration for the job.

  If you show that you really want to work there, why wouldn't they employ you?

- Never be late!

- Never try to make it seem like you know something when you don't.

  If you are being tested on your cocktail knowledge, simply say
  "I haven't had a chance to make one before".

  Don't try to make it up because it will make you look like a lying dufus.

What were some of the challenges you faced getting a Bartending job?
The fact that most bars are owned by men that would prefer to have young large breasted girls with little or no experience work at their bar than someone with more experience and no breasts whatsoever.

The Interview

What advice do you have for bartenders?

Be kind to your knees and wear shoes with heel supports in them.

You will thank me later for this advice.

What was your worst interviewing experience?

It was either the one where I was asked how to make a Gibson and I described a gimlet instead, or the one where during the 2nd interview process I saw the words "just so-so" written at the top of my resume.

Both of these, of course, were very early on in my illustrious bartending career. :)

What was your best interviewing experience?

The time I was asked to describe how to make a perfect Bourbon Manhattan, and the manager told me that I had been the only one of the interviewees to get it right.

What to do/bring/say?

Bring your A game. Make sure that there isn't anything that a manager can throw at you that you cannot answer or do.

What not to do/bring/say in an interview?

Copies of your resume, referral letters, and references....oh, and a winning personality!

Popular Questions Managers Will Ask?

A) Will you work day shifts?

B) Are you willing to barback/work the door, if need be?

C) How much are you expecting to make per hourly wage?

D) How much are you expecting to make in tips per shift?

E) How will you be getting to work?

Do you have a car or reliable means of transportation?

F) Have you been working behind a bar for long?

G) Why would you want to work at this particular bar?

Good Answers?

A) Yes.

B) Yes.

C) $5-$8

D) $150 minimum

E) I have a car, I live near reliable public transportation, I live within walking distance, etc.

F) Depends on whether you have or you haven't.

In either case, express how much you love the bar business.

G) Because I've been to this bar on both busy and slow nights, and I really like the vibe of the place and the people who come here.

I think I would be really happy working here.

Good Questions to ask them?

What would be my shift hours?

Do I receive a clothing allowance (if a uniform is required)

What is the tip-out rate?

Who do I need to tip? Who, if anyone, tips-out to me?

Is there a group insurance policy, or the possibility of

having one in the near future?
They Hire You. Now What?
10 Things to do/Ask before your first shift?

- Bring your own bar kit, just in case the bar doesn't have all of the items that you require (Make sure it is cool with management first).

- Is there an industry discount policy?

- Is there a comp key and what is the nightly limit?

- Can you sit at the bar after a shift?

- Are you allowed at the bar on your night off?

- Is there an employee discount?

- Who, if anyone, receives a free shift drink? (kitchen guys, management, etc.)

- If there are shift drinks, what are they allowed to drink?

- Make sure that you know the keg system and have access to backup bottles of spirit.

- Make sure that your bar is stocked up and you have all of your pars before the doors are open.

Your First Shift. Suggestions on how to do great?

- Be yourself.
- Make sure to always address your guests within 30 seconds of them sitting down, even if it is a head nod or a wave to acknowledge them
- Know your well spirits and study your drink list/menu.
- Have fun!

Adrian "Rocky" Noll – 6 years in the industry
www.MixologyMaddness.webs.com
A Creative Mixologist & Conceptual Artist which plays a large role in her innovative ideas for creating cocktails and formulating bar designs.

Her life as a bartender began in early 2008 and she has moved forward in the industry, starting a small private bartending business in the D.C., Maryland & Virginia area as well as traveled to different states working behind all types of bars from cruise ships and fine dining to Asian bistros and dive bars.
Rocky is currently living in California and working on a number of projects from fermenting fruits, distilling

brandy and going to school to become a Designer of All Things.

Rocky Says:
As you read through my experiences, you can see that when it comes to bartending there are a 100s of ways to utilize your skills and when you do, you see the advantages of it. When it comes to being "a great bartender" the same thing applies.

If you are reading this you might not be new to the Hospitality Industry but I'm guessing you are fairly new to the World of Bartending.

Let's start with the interview process.
During an interview a great bartender will do the following:

- Will show up to the interviews dressed in sync with the style of bar you are applying too.

- Be flexible with scheduling during the first few weeks/ months.

- Go in with the understanding that you are actually applying for a 'floating position' be prepared to be tossed, turned and thrown all around the schedule.

Kyle Branche - http://www.barprofessional.com
A 30-year veteran professional and private bartender in Los Angeles.

His wide variety of bar experiences in the City of Angels is second to none, having worked in many bars, nightclubs, private clubs, restaurants, hotels, concert venues, and is currently more off the grid today working a busy, yet more flexible schedule as a private on-call bartender with a variety of services, caterers, event planners, brand-sponsored events and private clientele working the party circuit, along with being the bar manager/bartender in 6 different establishments, while still holding position on-call in the bar at the famous Gardenia Room in Hollywood for 24 years.

"Working all over L.A. has given me the best experience that anyone can have and the best knowledge that anyone can gain".

His Blog of stories and encounters is culled from many moons behind the bar, now in his fourth decade, which has now produced a book series of stories and encounters: Vignettes over cocktails titled Life Behind Bars, with Books One and Two now available on Amazon.

Kyle was a contributing writer and columnist in the leading beverage magazines from 2002-2012, with 75 published pieces, including the monthly cocktail column "Liquid Kitchen" with Patterson's Beverage Journal (now

The Tasting Panel), feature cover stories, contributing articles, and ab online multimedia super feature story with Sante Magazine, titled "The Sleeping Spirit".

Kyle Says:
Job Search
Let the Hunting begin. (I'll use Los Angeles as an example) First of all, why wait for a job to come in from a school that's to work part-time in a tavern, when you would rather work in a hotel.

Begin your search for example, with all of the hotels in your surrounding area, and as far as you're willing to travel in one-way and /or round-trip mileage.

Choose your Theme Venues, and blanket the town, or towns.

Widen your range of thought, so you don't miss out on a job possibility.
And if you're open to re-location, then it expands that much more.

Always use:
Local newspapers – L.A. Times, Daily News, etc. employment section, and look under the 3 main categories: Bartenders, Hotels, and Restaurants.

Your local Job Service at the State EDD office or visit the on-line site.

In California, all jobs are on computer, so you can easily search through the whole state, and check out all the Bartending jobs available.

In research for this topic, every time I checked there were always jobs for bartenders. Take advantage of this free service to you.

Check out bar jobs on the internet / Check out www. headhunter.net

Check the Yellow Pages for all catering and banquet services, bartending services, hotel job hotlines, Word of mouth, and get to know some bar owners.
Check out: bartender.com, finediningjobs.com, wineandhospitalityjobs.com

Restaurant Connection – 275 5th St. – San Francisco, Ca. 94103 Phone – 415.777.1962 E-mail – restconnect@hotmail.com Jobs available in all aspects of the Restaurant/Food & beverage industry.
All levels of experience, casual to fine dining. Full-Time and Part-Time.

After you get hired, every once in a while, go out on other bar job interviews for good practice and experience, whether you need the job or not.

If the place is not looking for anybody, at least the manager gets to know your face for future reference. You'll be more relaxed.

Application

Most places require the filling out of a standard employment application, so in case you get hired on the spot, it's good to have some identification, social security card/number, and driver's license with you so the employer can make a copy of them.

If you don't have one or the other, they also accept a valid passport.

Fill the application out as much as possible, and above all, make your handwriting / penmanship as readable and nice looking as you can.

This shows something to the interviewer about your etiquette responsibility.
Maybe you count your change back to the customer as accurate as your writing.

If you do not think your writing is so good, go out and purchase the exact ballpoint
(thick or thin) in a pen that makes it look better.

Test them out and find the right one for you.
It's the little things that matter the most.

Résumé

If you have previous career experience in other occupations, use this to your advantage.

Managers love to work with and hire individuals with solid backgrounds in other fields as well, which is good for conversations of experiences for Bartender / customer relations.

Fill out the application, attach your resume of previous held positions in other occupations.

References
Personally and Professionally, have two or three references of each, in case prospective employers want to call and ask your friends and/or co-workers about you.

Not that it happens very much, but it's good to have with you in case the application requires it. People you know and trust will give the employer a more genuine understanding of you.

Phone Technique
Some places you initially call for work inquiry will give you more information than others.

Then again, there's only so many questions you can, and should ask anyway.
To make it quick and simple, call and ask:

1. **What Days and Hours do you accept applications?**
   If it feels and sounds comfortable, then say:

2. **I'm looking for Part-time or Full-time work, do you know if there's any available that I could apply for?**

At this point, they will usually ask: What position are you applying for?

Tell them, and they will then tell you either yeh or neh.

If they say yes we do,
You say: I'll put an application in, thank you for your time!

If they say no, not at this time,
You say: Thank you for your time!
Then go in at your earliest available time, and put in an application.

You could be speaking to the host or hostess, or it could be the manager.

Either way, use your best speaking voice, be kind and patient with response, and try to keep it quick and simple so in case their busy, you're not taking up too much of their time.

The best times to call depending on the venue and operation hours are:
9:00 am – 11:00 am and 2:30 pm – 4:30 pm

The "Inner-View"
As the prospective employee, your part of the talk is simple.

Trust your quality of presence.
Be calm, truthful, and simple.

Shift your energy to match the energy of the interviewer. Be them, so the rhythm is comfortable.

Questions the Interviewer might ask you, the prospective bartender.

1. "Can you work on holidays?"

2. "Do you plan to continue your education, and what are your plans for the future?"

3. "How far do you live from here?"

4. "How will you get to work?"

5. "When can you start work if you are hired?"

6. "Can you work days and nights, or split shifts?"

7. "Have you ever worked at night?"

8. "Are you familiar with setting up a Bar, mixes, garnishes etc.?"

9. "Did you ever work with or train a Barback?"

10. "What did you like and dislike about your last job?"

If the Interviewer notices that you have some experience, they might then ask:

11. "I see that you've worked for the last year at The Cascade Bar.

Why do you want to leave?"

12. "How much business did you do on a busy night?"

13. "How many Cocktail Servers did you handle?"

14. "What kind of cash register/transaction system did you work with?"

15. "What was your system of paying and collecting for the drinks you or your server sold?"

16. "How much did you pour?"

17. "Did you free pour, use a measured jigger or shot glass, or a liquor gun?"

18. "How did you handle Drunk customers?"

19. "How would you handle a customer complaining about you, another employee, or the way the bar is run?"

20. "What are the most important qualities, in your opinion, that make for a good bartender?"

Be positively aggressive in your interest of the position, but avoid at all costs looking desperate. This sends the wrong message. Be light about it all, yet eager to begin.

Is the Establishment right for you?
Let the interviewer talk about their Bar business, to give you a good basic idea of what goes on, the good and the less than good.

Have some questions for them as well; shifts, hours, benefits, insurance etc.
Not too many, but enough to show your interest, so you can also make your decision.

Bar Venue selection for work
If you have multiple choices of bar work in the area where you live, why not take advantage of the proper choice that can become the perfect fit for you to initially work in, before you move on to other themes to tend bar in, which allows growth and experience.

Certain energies and personalities work best with a particular theme/venue that could at this time be suitable for you to work in.

Managers hire on how you project yourself, so take this app-roach of looking for work if you have a selection to choose from.

If not, go with what you have available, and move forward with individual progress
from there.

What are The Best Ways to Ask For/Get a Raise, Promotion & Better Shifts?
Do the work better than anyone else, out-perform everyone, and if your boss is paying attention with any brains at all, you won't have to ask.

It is ultimately his/her (Boss) responsibility and in their job description.

If your boss is weak and playing favorites with other under-performing staff, don't waste your time.

Just know there is more turnover in management positions than that of the hourly staff. This industry causes its own problems, and then turns around and wonders why it has them!

If you're a manager, what advice can you give to employees?

Managers today for the most part have their bonuses connected to the bottom line, which is a conflict of interest.

Good luck in squeezing out anything above the minimum wage these days.

Become so valued that they can't risk losing you.

However, it's more important to go for getting better shifts that increase your income through tips via business volume than it is to try and get a raise on your hourly that potentially takes money out of a manager's pocket.

You will get more from the former than you will from the latter.

Bartending as your Social Life

Many bartenders utilize the occupation as a comfortable way to communicate with others from all walks.

If you keep it light, the bar is a good practicing springboard, and again is part of your job. It can create the extroversion balance to a natural introversion tendency, if this is part of your character and personality trait.

This works beautifully, and after a swamped night of bar business, when you get home, the last thing you'll want is to hear or have to listen to anything.

Verbal communication at a consistent level takes a lot of energy, and you will notice how valuable your quiet time will be to you after a while.

Work around the world
Bartending is the perfect job for you.
Get to know anyone and everyone, and work abroad.

Listen, Learn, Absorb, and Expand.
If you get the chance, don't forget you can transfer to places all over the world, provided you're employed with a chain that has business operations in other countries, and if you're single or unmarried and no strings to hold you back, then you're free to do so.

Take advantage of it, even if just for a period of time, say a year or two.

Make sure your passport and other necessary papers are in order ahead of time, so you have a smooth transition. This gives you the opportunity to learn different languages, and make many new friends.

Brian Dougherty
Ten years in the Restaurant and Bar industry with the majority of this with the Keg Steakhouse and Bar as a Manager.

I have participated in over 1,000 interviews in my career and am currently the operating partner of one of BC's largest Landscape Construction and Maintenance companies.

Brian Says:
How to Create a Great Resume?
Personally drop it off with the individual whom is in charge of the hiring for this position and go to whatever level required to do so.

Putting a face to a resume will go a long ways.

Make sure you dress the part and get ready for an interview on the spot as this could very well happen if you catch them at the right time.

The resume should include a reference letter from a previous employer or industry colleague.

Jazz it up with nice paper and sleeves so it sticks out from the rest.
Make sure to include any articles or blogs about any events you were part of.

5 Things to include
- Contact info for Great phone references of previous employers or colleagues.

- Only include long term employment history and avoid putting down the small side jobs so it doesn't look like you bounce around.

- Cover letter made out to the place of employment and why you want to join their team.

- All schooling and courses
- All awards and accolades.

5 Big Mistakes to avoid
- Correct e-mail and current phone numbers
  (don't make the mistake of including an old number/e-mail!)

- Don't have any employment gaps.
  If you had a lot of jobs during one particular year trying to find stability, put down the one job you held the most that year and include that one as the job you held for that year.

Don't specify the timeline, just include the year.

- Do not fax it
- Check with your references to make sure they are giving you a top notch reference.

- Do not include previous employers that would say no to rehiring you no matter the reason they would not.

- Do not include a general introduction.
  Make sure it is specific to that position and company you are applying with so it doesn't just look like you are broadcasting your resume to every place in town.

 **Guy Lafitte** – Over 30 years' experience. Been behind the sticks at everything from cowboy bars to craft bars.

I'm always looking to improve the art… researching old cocktail books taking cocktail and cooking classes, even teaching classes at my local community center.

Had a traveling show for a while where I went from place to place doing magic Bartending.

I'm still behind the stick at a historic hotel in MN where I've instituted a historical cocktail a day.
Why? Why not?

I've been crafting cocktails before the classics where considered classics.
And I figure folks could learn from some of my experiences.

My grandfather, who taught me, always said to pass the knowledge on.

Guy Says:
5- How to Create a Great Resume?
Make it yours but make it theirs too.

I've seen far too many generic resumes.
When i've been in the hiring position I look for personality in the resume.

Craig's List has increased the number of resumes one gets and you want your resume to stand out.
I've included two of my unusual but successful resumes below.

6- Things to include In Your Resume

1) Your successes but with facts and figures.

2) Training and work experience.
I like to see if a bartender has gone the extra mile ...
Advanced cocktail classes,
Cooking classes,
Sales/Management classes.

3) A professional email address, not something like sexytramp@gmail.com .
(don't try this, it may be taken ☺)..
Use your name.

4) Tell me what you could do for me, my bar and my guests.

5) A current phone number and <u>make sure your greeting isn't too off the wall</u>

7- Big Mistakes to avoid

1) A goofy or unprofessional email address.

2) Trying to inflate your experience ...
Especially if you can't talk the talk in a job interview.

3) Telling me that you're applying for the bartending job - that's a given.

4) Don't hand over a resume that has been updated in ink – Scratching out your old phone number and writing in your new one.

5) Too many pages.

8- Examples/Stories of great Resumes?

I'm partial to creative types.

I received one that was in the shape of a cocktail glass. The young lady put a lot of work into it.

Unfortunately she didn't match her resume. Her experience was more than a little inflated.

9- Examples/Stories of Terrible Resumes

The worst resume I received was handwritten on yellow legal paper.

When I first received it, I looked at it quickly and hoped it was created on a computer and would have considered it creative but when I was able to get a good look at it

I saw it was handwritten with words scratched out and misspellings.

The Interview -
11- What advice do you have for bartenders?
Be prepared.
Visit the bar ahead of time.
Research them on the internet.

Know what kind of beer and cocktails the serve and know something about those drinks.

That way you can gear your answers at the interview towards the products they sell.

I've cut many an interview short when we talk about wine and the interviewee doesn't know what varietal means.

12- What were some of the challenges you faced getting a Bartending job?
Only over the past ten years have I been facing challenges ... and it's the age one.

In Las Vegas if I heard the words "you know this is an under 40 club" or if they asked for an 8X10 shot of me in a bathing suit, I knew that the interview would be it.

It's then I set my sights on different bars and venues where my age and style would be an asset.

13- What was your worst interviewing experience?
When I interviewed at a chain restaurant and I wasn't asked anything about being a bartender other than how long have I been a bartender.

I answered, "I've been behind the sticks for over 30 years ... "She had no idea what I was talking about.

When I tried to steer the interview towards my bar experience and the bar there it was apparent she new nothing about the bar.

She was front of house lead.
I cut the interview short because I felt it was a waste of time.

14- What was your best interviewing experience?
I walked into the room and was introduced to one of the owners - the other one was out of town.

He started the interview with,
"You ever worked Capitol Hill. My business partner and his wife used to go to this bar there and the guy makes great drinks and does some magic too. Had a mustache like yours. The bar is closed now. My partner said that's the person I should hire."

I answered - "I'm the guy"
The interview ended that quickly.
Hand shake and I got the job.

15- What to do/bring/say?

If you've done the research then it will be easy.
Tell them what you can do for them.

If you have press cuttings - bring them. I have a portfolio that speaks of my professionalism as a bartender and manager.

When I decided to put this one together and use it, I got two job offers.

This is not a typical portfolio but from beginning to end it is geared towards how my skills will benefit their bar/ restaurant.

I have to customize parts of it for each job but it was well worth it.

I also have a leave behind packet which includes...
A resume,
A mini resume on a large index card,
My press clippings,
Pertinent awards,
Training Certificates and a business card.

I always carry the mini resume and the business card when I'm job hunting.
You just never know.

16- What not to do/bring/say in an interview?

Cell phone. Friends or parents. Your pet.

17- Popular Questions Managers Will ask?

Have you ever been to our bar?

Tell me about your experience.

Once you've gone on a couple interviews you'll know the common questions.

18- Good Answers?

If you have researched the bar or restaurant and were honest on your resume then the answers will come easy.

Think of the questions yourself and practice answers.

19- Good Questions to ask them?

The most important question,
I feel,
is at the end of the interview
Ask for the job.

Scott Says:

I think its a fantastic point Guy. I never even thought of that. It's so obvious it's brilliant!

Just like inviting your guest to come back again when they leave.

What exact words would you say?

Maybe list a few options…

ie. Thanks very much for your time "name of person". I'd very much like to work for you.

Hmmm, I'm just waking up but i'm amused at myself that I'm having trouble actually finding the words to "ask" for the job....
so, by the way, do I get the job?
Can I have the job?

Guy Says:
In Seattle at the end of the interview I was told they would making a decision in a couple of days. I told them point blank that I was the bartender they were looking for and to prove it I would come in and work a shift for free.

They said that they weren't open yet (the job posting was on Craigslist and the interview was at a junior college - it was all hush hush).

I replied I'd come in and do some scud work.
They thanked me for my time and shooed me out the door.
I figured I maybe was too forceful. I walked to my car and drove away.

Must have been ten minutes later when my cell rang.
Not only did I get the job but I was made head bartender and FOH lead.

The first time I used it was in Miami. It was a good interview and a lot of joking around so when I was asked if I had any questions I replied,
"Can I have the job?"
The manager of the place returned "can you start tomorrow?"

When I started the next day he told me that he hired because I asked for the job.

Every interview I've gone on I've asked for the job. How I ask is dependent on the flow of the interview - Sometimes I offer to work a shift for free but that's usually for non-corporate type places.

I won't say it works all the time but its a sales close technique - you're asking for the sale - and part of your job as a bartender is sales - in this case you're selling yourself.

Guy

Scott Says: When you look at these resumes, who wouldn't be super impressed and at the very least give him an interview or even hire him on the spot?
Thanks a ton Guy. I hope to sit at your bar one day.

P.S. Below are three resumes I've used in over 10 years to some success.

The first two are more whimsical.
The Western theme I used at various places throughout the west.

GUY LAFITTE
LAFITTE@DRLAFITTE.COM
702-274-1881

FOCUS
To provide excellent & entertaining services to the guests at Cactus!

CLASSIC COCKTAIL MIXOLOGIST WITH A TWIST OF MAGIC

- 20+ Years Experience
- Highly Motivated
- Enthusiastic Team Player

- Dynamic Leadership Personality
- Sales and Management Skills
- Windows/MAC/POS Literate

BAR EXPERIENCE
Abridged

Bartender, Food Team
Seattle, WA 2011/Las Vegas, NV 2008
Seasonal bartending for corporate and special events

Magic Bartender, Big Nose Kate's
Tombstone, AZ 2002-2004
Worked behind the bar doing magic bartending for mostly a tourist crowd

Bartender, The Beach
Las Vegas, NV 2001-2002
Worked part time for the convention and corporate crowd

Bartender/Entertainer, Wayward
Phoenix, AZ 1996-2001
Bartending and entertainment at catered events and corporate functions

Magic Bartender, Diamond Lil's
Scottsdale, AZ 1998-2000
Worked part-time doing magic bartending at a cowboy bar for locals & tourists

Bartender, Big Daddy's Lounges
South Florida 1982-1987
Worked at various lounges that catered to everything from bikers to disco divas

OTHER EXPERIENCE

Have Magic Will Travel
1993-Present
My own magical entertainment company

Bartender Training
ABC Bartending School *1982, 2011*
BarSmarts Wired *2010*

HIGHLIGHTS

Educational
Associate of Arts in Criminology
Honorary Doctorate

Miscellaneous
US Navy Diver
Award Winning Speaker

Class 12 Mixologist and Food Worker Permits

REFERENCES AVAILABLE UPON REQUEST
HAVE BAR TOOLS WILL TRAVEL

The Tiki theme was used in Las Vegas.

OBJECTIVE

To provide excellent & entertaining service to the guests at your establishment

BAR EXPERIENCE

Magic Bartender, Big Nose Kate's Tombstone, AZ 2003-2004

Worked behind the bar doing magic & mixing drinks for mostly a tourist crowd

Bartender, The Beach, Las Vegas, NV 2002

Worked part-time days for the convention & corporate crowd

Bartender/Entertainer, WayWardWind, Phoenix, AZ 1996-2001

Worked & entertained at catered events for both U.S. & International clients

Magic Bartender, Diamond Lil's Scottsdale, AZ 1998-1999

Worked part-time at the main bar, a cowboy bar for tourists & locals

Bartender, Big Daddy's Lounges South Florida 1982-1986

Started as a bouncer & worked my way up to bartender

OTHER EXPERIENCE

Entertainment - Have Magic Will Travel, 1993 to present

My own magic & entertainment company

Gaming - Knight of the Green Cloth Enterprises, 1993 to present

My own gaming consultancy, where I teach games, game protection & lecture on the history of gambling

EDUCATION

ABC Bartending School (refresher course), Las Vegas, NV 2008
Southwest Missouri State, Honored with a Doctorate 1999
Florida International University, Journalism 1983-1984
ABC Bartending School (original course) 1982
Miami-Dade Community College, AA Criminology 1976

References available upon request

This bottom one is the more professional.

GUY LAFITTE
(651) 243-0322 / guy@guylafitte.com

BARTENDER

To provide an excellent experience for the guests at your establishment

SKILLS SUMMARY

Over twenty years experience in both the entertainment and the food and beverage industry

- Efficient, Fast and Friendly
- Entertaining and Knowledgable
- Enthusiastic Team Player
- Customer Service Oriented
- Sales and Management Skills
- Money Handling Experience
- Strong Work Ethic
- POS: Aloha, Micros, NCR, PointOS

PROFESSIONAL EXPERIENCE

Bartender—Classically trained mixologist. Worked in everything from fast-paced tourist bars, night clubs and restaurants to Officer's Clubs and cowboy bars. Also tended bar at weddings, private parties and corporate events

- Used my skill set as a bartender to make Bako the #2 bar in Seattle according to Eater.com
- Able to mix ingredients, such as liquor, soda, water and juices to prepare cocktails and other drinks
- Skilled in anticipating, identifying and fulfilling the customer's needs
- Able to handle all aspects of opening and closing including prep work, stocking of alcohol and related supplies, and cash counting with daily and weekly receipts running between $500 to $15,000
- Experienced in craft, classic cocktails and magic bartending
- Created custom and themed cocktails and cocktail menus
- Trained in the recognition of intoxicated patrons and the proper procedures necessary to limit problems and stop patrons from excessive drinking

Server—Duties include set up, table service (buffet to full service) including wine service, table clearing and room reset

- Served predetermined meals and took food and beverage orders from patrons
- Worked events up to and exceeding 750 people

Entrepreneur—Owned and operated what started as Western-themed entertainment company that grew to add training programs in sales, management and table games training

- Private party and corporate event bartending usually in character: Western, Magic, Rude
- Gambling style entertainment at festivals and corporate events ~ over 2000 performances
- Master of Ceremonies and Poker Tournament Host including organizing casino nights
- Conducted seminars in Sales, Management and Time Management
- Instructed casino personnel in table games and game protection

CAREER HIGHLIGHTS

Bako, Seattle ~ Bar Manager/FOH Lead
ɔodz/Herban Feast Catering/Allegiance Staffing/Food
Team, Seattle, Las Vegas ~ Bartender/Server
The Beach, Las Vegas ~ Bartender
Big Nose Kate's, Tombstone ~ Bartender
Diamond Lil's, Scottsdale ~ Bartender
Big Daddy's Lounges, South Florida ~
"The McDonald's of Bars" ~ Bartender
KGC Enterprises, LLC ~ Owner

EDUCATION AND HONORS

Associate of Arts in Criminology ~
Miami-Dade Community College
Hon. **Doctorate** ~ South West Missouri State
BarSmarts ~ Pernod Ricard, 2010
Advanced Bartending School, 1982
Certified Sales and Management Trainer ~ CareerTrac
Award Winning Speaker
US Navy Diver/PADI Scuba Instructor

"Have Bartools Will Travel"

Head bartender Guy Lafitte provides the best reason to visit Bako
Hanna Raskin, Food Critic/Seattle Weekly

<u>**Yelp Reviews**</u>

I'm 43, I've never in my life experienced a better bartender than Guy at Bako. What a shock that was. He has been around. I've been drinking Martinis for years but tonight I feel like I had one for the first time. - Peter R

The cocktails are what bumped this review up to three stars. They were inventive, expertly mixed and the cocktail menu was well-presented and even a little poetic. Just come for drinks and you'll probably have more fun than I did. - Hai Yen

We sat at the bar and got great service from both Guy (the bartender) . . - Jenna

I must mention that Guy the Bartender was such a charming character! (His mustache is simply mesmerizing!) He is well-traveled and has very interesting stories to tell you. I did not order any cocktails, but he was mixing up some beautiful drinks.
If you go to Bako, sit at the bar and chat with Guy! - Yamiko

We went into Bako for their drinks, and ended up getting some of their foursies happy hour food. To start, the craft cocktails were awesome! And Guy the bartender gave us a little history behind each of his creations. This man really knows his alcohol. I recommend having a manhattan or a floridita! - Mike

It's not hard to find someone to sing Guy's (the head bartender) praises, and the man deserves it. Not only can he make a mean cocktail, his service is prompt, warm, and entertaining. What more can you ask for in a bartender? My favorite cocktail is a Manhattan, and Guy's grandfather's recipe makes it all the better. He even barrel-ages his own cocktails--ask him about his Agin' Cajun and Jean Harlow. And when you're contemplating on what you want for your fourth or fifth drink of the night, just let Guy do the deciding for you--you won't be disappointed. - Sammi

I've been here twice, now, and have had a great experience both times. The last time I was here I started with a cocktail, ordering the Manhattan (with rye whiskey). It was prepared deliciously and served with a brandy-soaked cherry. Very delicious. - Doug

Solid bar and a fun bartender. - Ian

They had a bartender there who was excellent and had the highest standards. I think he is gone now, but i hope his polish rubbed off on the others. - Jaques

There have been more than a few times that I've sent out both a whimsical and professional.

Yes, it got me the interview and in three cases a job.

 **Scott Says:** "One of the best people, and bartenders, I've ever known. I've learned a lot from this smiling guy."

Chris Simone - Approximately 27 years in the service industry. I'm Chris Simone, General Manager of Weinkeller, Niagara Falls Canada. www.weinkeller.ca

I paid my dues Bussing at Bert N Ernie's Toronto 1987-1990. I finished there as a Server and came out West to pay my dues, delivering pizza, cooking, bussing, odd jobs, sometimes three at once.

Got a break and got hired at Uptown Charlie's across the street from the Coliseum where the Vancouver Canucks played. I paid my dues and learned to move fast for pre-and post-game rushes. I moved downtown with the Canucks, opening The Shark Club Bar and Grill, a wild pre-game, post-game, night club, Sports Bar.

And after four full years of bartending at the hottest Sports bar in Vancouver, Canada, I made myself available and was hired at The Roxy Cabaret.

I worked beside Scott Young and all the rest of them. I wasn't a Casanova, although my hands were fast and my smile wide. I spent three years at the Roxy. So that's 10 years of full-time bartending, alongside going to school and being in other businesses.

Then I went out in to the traditional business world and mainly focused on my construction company and did a lot of part-time staff training for restaurants, bars and customer service/life skills arenas.

In 2013, I joined up with Weinkeller, a food and wine craftery out of Niagara Falls. In the position of General Manager, I am allowed to do what I love.

The staff feel like fellow campers at a high-end campsite. The guests are over the top with reactions and feedback, so it is good. My job is to keep the flow in around and through Weinkeller as a Niagara Falls landmark.

Chris Says:
What Increases The Odds Of A Bartender Getting Hired?
You must have persistence.

You must know who is reading your resume. Just ask when you drop it off then make an educated guess at when he/she might answer the phone.

For sure at cash out, an hour before open etc. then call and introduce yourself and that's it.

You can obviously mention your eagerness to get employment, but this call is not for that, it's an introduction.

After that meet in person and find out what he/she wants and communicate your values in terms of his/her values.

That is all. Be vulnerable and honest.

How to Choose Which Bars To Apply At?
Where a lot of people go or have the potential to go. Apply at a place that you might have only yourself to serve, or a large section, so there is potential to maximize your shifts. Avoid tired old timer type places.

How to Create a Great Resume?
Picture, one page, references upon request

Making a great cover letter?
Greet, rapport, needs, confirm needs, solutions, close.

What were some of the challenges you faced getting a Bartending job?
Talking to the right person in person

The Interview
What advice do you have for bartenders?
Don't sit so straight, loosen up.
Speak well, eye contact, don't touch your hair or face.
Listen and ask questions, remember what's important to interviewer.

What not to do/bring/say in an interview?
Don't try to get friendly. Be low maintenance.

Popular Questions Managers Will ask?
What do you care about.

Good Answers?
The truth

Good Questions to ask them?
What is the mission Statement?
Room for future advancement?
What he/she likes to see In a server

They Hire You. Now What?
Things to do/Ask before your first shift?
Time, uniform, what door to enter who to report to.
Nothing else, low maintenance.

Your First Shift. Suggestions on how to do great?
Just figure out your position and what it includes.

Don't ask too many questions, be a sponge.
Hopefully it will be busy so you can get a snapshot of
everything working together.
At the end of the shift ask about your next shift and what I
can do to be better.

That's it, low maintenance.
Do not hang around after your first shift.
Give them a chance to talk about you. Either way it's good.

Christopher Sinclair
I've been a bartender for almost 11 years now. I've worked everything from clubs to lounges, from dive bars to hotel bars, from fine dining to not-so-fine dining. I've attended bartending school and subsequently taught at the same bartending school years later for about four years.

I've placed and won multiple local & national (U.S.) competitions. I run a consulting company. Currently president of the Sacramento chapter of the U.S. Bartender's Guild.

Christopher Says:
What Increases The Odds Of A Bartender Getting Hired?
Personality, Personality, Personality.

I can teach any schmuck to make drinks and do it well. I can't, on the other hand, teach you not to be a prick or have a work ethic.

Specifically, I look for someone who is self-confident without too much ego.
And some one HONEST!
How to Choose Which Bars To Apply At?
I always tell my students and friends to first invest the time to find a bar or restaurant that they actually like first.

Spend time and the space and actually expend
some effort dissecting what they like and what they don't.

Next imagine spending eight hours a day, 6 days a week in
that environment.

If that's all good, then that's the place for you, otherwise,
don't waste the time of others, and most importantly
your own time trying to get a job that will only make
you miserable.

Plus, when you actually find a place you do enjoy, your
enthusiasm will come through to the hiring manager and
hopefully eventually to your guests.

How to Create a Great Resume?
There are many differing thoughts on resumes. And sorry to
say, but you simply can't please everyone. The things that
will intrigue and excite certain people, will offend others.
That being said, I do have a few tips.

1) **Avoid lengthy sentences.**
    Managers usually just scan your info on a resume, forcing
    them to read more will usually only irritate them. Use
    bullet points to make your resume "scan-able".

2) **Include some non-industry interests.** This will provide
    some authentic insight to your personality, and just maybe
    give you a point of interest that can offer a connection to
    the hiring manager or another employee (i.e. ex-soldiers
    love other ex-soldiers)

3) This is debatable, but **I usually suggest adding a photo** (or two or three).

One must be very selective, remember, this is for a JOB. Only choose "goofy" photos if they are applicable. Use photos that show you doing your job, as well as photos that offer a view into your personality.

More than anything though, know that this photo(s) is going be all that anyone knows about you until they actually get a chance to get to know you (and yes, they will judge you from your photos). But when restaurants and bars receive hundreds of resumes, this is the best way to help ensure that your resume is attached to you.

Oh, and choose a photo with you smiling.

5 Big Mistakes to avoid
Avoid too many job descriptions in your resume that aren't the industry you are applying for.

I can't tell you many times I've received resumes from people clearly trying to get an "in-between" job.

Unless the bar or restaurant clearly is seasonal (i.e. a beach town or a ski resort), most likely the hiring manager doesn't want to have to hire you just to hire someone else in two or three months.

Find a place that is actually going to work for you and the person that hires you. This way you won't have to burn any bridges.

Avoid talking shit about previous jobs. I won't hire someone who lacks tact and class. We all have those horror stories, and we can share them over a beer, not a resume.

Making a great cover letter?
Cover letters should be unique to the specific bar you are applying for.

If you choose to flyer a city with your resume, don't include a cover letter.

A cover letter is a great way to include your personality and your excitement and passion since it's impossible to do that on a resume.

Think of it as your handshake before actually meeting someone.

The Interview
What advice do you have for bartenders?
I have pretty simple rules when it comes to interviews, and it applies to both or all people involved in the interview process; be legit, and be yourself.

This is a conversation, no more.

Look people in the eye, answer and ask questions honestly, and don't devalue yourself.

Remember good bars need good bartenders and much as good bartenders need good bars. And yes, both are rare.

That being said, don't be cocky and allow yourself to admit you don't have all the answers (again this goes for everyone in the conversation).
I personally don't have patience for the "yes sir/ no sir" mentality of managing or service. I am a server, not a servant.

This is an important distinction and one that gets clarified during the interview process.
I don't hire people that compromise themselves for the customer either.

> When you are a bartender,
> most of the time it is important
> that
> you are the captain of the ship,
> whether you cut someone off,
> disrupt an argument,
> or better yet,
> simply set the tone of your bar for a night.

Bartenders need to be self-assured and not wimps (entitlement is also a clear sign of weakness of character by the way).

What is the best way to ask/ get a promotion or for a raise?
I've never received a raise (outside of working corporate and getting a contractually obligated raise which amounted to twenty five cents more an hour each year... wooooo!) I don't really see a reason to get one given normal circumstances for just being good at your job.

Now if you end up doing more than simply bartending or serving, then sure.

For instance, if a bartender were to take over inventory and ordering, and it takes time out of your normal week to handle this, then yes ask.

If you get a no as an answer, start looking for a better place to work and let them find someone else to work for free.

Similarly, if you move into a management or supervisor position, do the math.

Remember that this is rarely an actual increase in pay.

Make sure that you are getting compensated for the time and effort as you won't be making tips anymore.

Daryl Brice
I've been bartending for over 20 years, 15 of them in nightclubs and five years in pubs and restaurants. I've also been a Head Bartender, Manager and a GM. Most of my experience has been in high-volume establishments, bartending in some of the most popular nightclubs (The Roxy with Scott Young), bars, pubs and music festivals.

Every place I've worked for more than a couple years I've set the highest sales record.

As a GM I helped turn a downtown nightclub around resulting in doubling the value of the business within two years.

Daryl Says:
What Increases The Odds Of A Bartender Getting Hired?
Most of the great jobs I've had, came from knowing people.

You need to introduce yourself and get to know the people in your local hospitality industry. Talk to people in the industry, ask them questions and get their advice.

The Interview
What advice do you have for bartenders?
It's mostly about personality, be yourself, be honest.

If you're nervous or excited, let them know.
Tell them your feel that way because you really want to work there and do a great job.

What was your worst interviewing experience?
One time I was in a second interview and the GM didn't really want to hire someone from outside of the company.

I found this out later but he asked me some awkward questions and I gave some awkward answers.

I told the guy that I had the first interview with that I thought I just gave the worse interview ever. That's when he told me the GM wanted to promote from within.

Don't sweat a bad interview, just move on to the next one. A lot of this process can be out of your control. You need to accept that.

Good Questions to ask them?
At the end interview I like to ask them in a friendly half joking way "so when do I start?"

Your First Shift. Suggestions on how to do great?
The first shift is all about getting the lay of the land.

Be a sponge and take in as much as you can.

You're not going to remember everything so don't be afraid to ask again and again if needed. I find it takes two weeks to feel a little bit comfortable and month or two to start feeling really good and confident. It's a process.

Scott Christian
My name is Scott Christian and I have 14 years in the industry. I began tending bar in 2004. I began at TGI Friday's in 2003 as a server and was promoted to the bar shortly after my 21st birthday. I first competed in the Friday's World Bartender Championship in 2010, making my first world final in 2012.

Beyond Friday's I have competed in flair bartending competitions all over the country and Canada. I have wins on the FBA Pro Tour Advanced Division and the Toronto Flair League B Division.

In addition to my experience as a flair bartender, I am now the manager of the six bars open to the public at the Western and Southern Financial Open professional tennis tournament in Mason, OH. I meet with sponsors, write the schedules, aid in bar design, manage inventory, and keep the bars running during the eight-day stretch with attendance approaching 200,000 people.

Scott Says:
What Increases The Odds Of A Bartender Getting Hired?
Radiating confidence!
Confidence for a bartender is one of the most important "tools" in his or her arsenal.

Confidence often is a result of experience, self-worth, and natural personality.
All of these are traits of a great bartender!

How to Choose Which Bars To Apply At?
Choose a bar that fits your personality, one of the best parts of being a bartender is personality is encouraged, you don't just get to be yourself, you HAVE to be yourself!

Also, find out about the areas you want to apply, is it an up and coming area with potential for more places to open? Growing areas and increased competition isn't bad for a good bar, it brings more people to that area and they will find the best spots.

Does the bar "fit in" with the crowd that patronizes that area?

Does the business rely on tourism, is it seasonal, or is the basis regulars?

How to Create a Great Resume?
Be brief, nobody wants to read a novel, so a nice design and an introduction that pops. You want to be able to be the first resume in the stack and still be remembered by the last resume.

Big Mistakes to avoid
Too wordy
Poor grammar
False claims

Making a great cover letter?
A great cover letter is concise and is personalized. Do your homework; find out some things about the company, finding out who will be receiving your letter or who is in charge of hiring/setting up interviews is a great place to start.

The Interview
What advice do you have for bartenders?
Avoid saying negative things about the place or places you have come from. We all have things that we feel could be done better in the bars we work in, and the hiring manager doesn't want to hear about how poorly managed or staffed your previous job was.

What was your worst interviewing experience?
I was coming off of a terrible St. Patrick's Day weekend, we were short on glassware, we ran out of vital product, and overall was a poorly prepared for weekend.

So as you could imagine, I was very upset. I had an interview the following week, and I feel like some of my frustrations came out in the interview. That is something you don't want, because at any bar or restaurant can have a bad weekend or a mix up in ordering, it is important to understand these things and show that you are able to work your way through it.

What was your best interviewing experience?
There was a change in management at my seasonal bartending job so I was unsure if I still had a job. So I went in and interviewed for the job I already had.

During the interview I expressed some ideas I had to improve our operation and was given a pay raise and asked to consult with the bar set ups.

Through the following weeks of planning I was given another raise and ended up being promoted to bar manager.

What to do/bring/say?
Dress for success, bring your personality, and don't try to over sell yourself.
Be modest but confident.

What not to do/bring/say in an interview?
A bad or overly smug attitude.

Popular Questions Managers Will ask?
The question I find that trips people up is, "what is your greatest weakness?"

Good Answers?

Be prepared to answer this question, not in the sense of a "weakness" but, "an area I feel I would like to improve on is…"

Good Questions to ask them?

Is there mission statement or vision statement for the bar/ company?

Remember not all bars are created equal, you don't want to go in to a failing bar, if they do not have goals for the future, what is the benefit of working for them?

They Hire You. Now What?
10 Things to do/Ask before your first shift?

1. Learn specialty drink recipes.
2. Learn the beers.
3. Learn the wines.
4. Learn the spirit and cordial list.
5. Ask what drinks are popular or on special.
6. When and what are special nights.
7. What type of POS is used?
8. What shifts will you work?
9. What, if any, offerings are on the food menu?
10. If you are relocating, find out the alcohol and tobacco laws in that city or state.

Your First Shift. Suggestions on how to do great?
My advice is to be observant, find the stand out employees and see what they do that makes them stand out.

Listen, listen, listen!
You don't want to come in smug with a "know it all" attitude. This will not get you far with the employees and if you don't win over the employees, your chances of winning over the regulars are bleak.

Jancy Nightingale – 4 years in the industry.
I am a proactive graphic designer and inspired mixologist working towards fusing the two into a sales / marketing career.

Jancy Says:
What are The Best Ways to Ask For/Get a Raise, Promotion & Better Shifts?
Actions speak louder than words.
SHOW them you deserve the upgrade.

At my first job, I proved to have the strongest sales of the group, so I was rewarded an extra shift. I'm currently not in a setup where this situation would occur, but I'd say it's ultimately in your hands.

Do the work, build your patron base and if you work for a good establishment, they'll see your contribution and reward you accordingly.

Alexey Balashov

More than 10 years of experience in the bar industry. Experience in different kinds of bars such as the bar in the restaurants, the lobby bars at the hotels, a pubs, a bars at a nightclubs.

Studied for a variety of professional programs big brands (Bols luquers,Absolut, Bacardi, Finland, Midori, etc.) Worked with brands Bols, Jonny Walker, Bacardi. Winner of multiple championships of bartenders art around the world.

More than 2,000 performances in competitions and commercial shows around the world. Creator projects Bala Show – professional flair show and Dance Flair Show – eccentric bartenders show.

My big passion is flair bartending, but it is a second!

First for me is a customer service!

Alexey Says:
What Increases The Odds Of A Bartender Getting Hired?
Accurate, observation, responsiveness, memory, diligence, communicability

How to Choose Which Bars To Apply At?
You must select the style that suits you.
If you like a calm and quiet atmosphere, then this is a restaurant.
If you are an energetic person, select a nightclub.
If you want to experiment in the field of cocktails, select mixology bar etc.

In any case, try to get in your life experience in different styles.

How to Create a Great Resume?
The biggest secret summary:

Brevity – No unnecessary words, incomprehensible acronyms and terms;

Activity – The need to use active verbs that show activity. For example, if you only have a basic knowledge of flair bartending, and they are required for this position, you must write "basic level of flair bartending."

Selectivity – Involves careful selection of information
Do not try to fit everything into a single summary.

Remember, the resume must fully correspond to the position for which you are applying for!

Mistakes to avoid
Discrepancy in employment history, education, experience, challenger objective requirements of the job or the employer will expose it.

Too short resume – it is not clear whether the author has nothing to say about himself, whether you're a shy grey mouse, afraid to speak up.

Demonstration of frequent change jobs without giving objective reasons;

Too-detailed summary containing a lot of unnecessary information,
and lyrical digressions or manifestations of inappropriate humor.

Making a great cover letter?
If the person is writing a cover letter, stress that it was written for this company, and does not send this cover letter to "all."

This shows that he is really interested in working for this specific employer.

What advice do you have for bartenders?
You need to work where you want to work. If you do not like the concept of establishment, the people with whom you work, where you serve guests etc.
Find the courage to change your job.

And a new job should meet your requirements.

Work should be fun and develop you into a professional.

Prepare for the interview, this is very important.
Most of the bartenders are not prepared for the interview.

What were some of the challenges you faced getting a Bartending job
Lack of experience in the initial stage
Low pay
Inconvenient work schedule
Unsuccessful bar format

What was your worst interviewing experience?
I was interviewed a few hours and did not get the job because of the young age.

What was your best interviewing experience?
The interview lasted 1 minute. Unforgettable.

What to do/bring/say?
Determine the specific purpose of your interview – a position (the bartender, bar manager, etc.

When you will came in for an interview, you should know what you want from this interview, why you want to get a job for this job, etc.

Do not go for a job interview, "without a goal".
It is instantly recognized by an experienced interviewer.

Find out as much information about the job and the bar, club or company.

Study the job description, the requirements that the employer makes available for this job, it will help you give clear examples of the duties you performed in a previous job, and what have the necessary skills. Next, you need to get as much information about the bar in which you are going on a job interview.

Pay attention to the appearance and the simple rules of etiquette!

Impression of you before and after the interview.
You need to come in for an interview for 15-20 minutes before your appointment.

This is the time you may need to bring myself up to talk to the security or the secretary of the reception.

Be welcoming and friendly to all employees of the company. At the end of the interview thank the interviewer for the interview conducted.

Show you're proactive stance on this job!

The best thing that you can tell us about yourself, to be sold to the employer.

Do not hesitate to show your strong desire to work in this company, to achieve high results. By this point to pay special attention to young bartenders.

Think about your motivation to work, the thrust!

Prepare for the question
"Why do you want this position?
What do you want to achieve success in your career?"

When answering the questions, "your career goals" appropriate response would be "for the near future, I'd like you to offer me this job ."

Prepare for yourself-presentation!
Get ready for a story about yourself, as this question will necessarily be specified.

Well, if you have a folder available on self-presentation, especially for young bartenders. Begin to build this folder at the very start of your training. There, you put your professional CV (resume), copies of diplomas, certificates that you had a chance to get.

At the interview you will have a lot to say about yourself, but the self-presentation folder will help you not to be unfounded in this sensitive issue.

Do not speak ill of a former employer!

Perhaps needless to say but you should not be late. It is better to arrive 10 minutes earlier to a little "come to your senses," calm down, look around the office.

And then to go directly to the interviewer.

If you were late, then do not despair:
Just briefly apologize to the interviewer, without resorting to unnecessary explanations. Do not knock before you come into the office.

First, it is not included in the rules of business etiquette, and secondly, it will give your self-doubt .

When prompted to sit down, choose the most comfortable place to sit down and try so that your position does not constitute an obstacle between you and the interviewer.

Try not to get nervous and stay with dignity.

Remember, you are not on the exam and the interviewer is also interested in you as you are in the job.

After all, if you are called for an interview, then, as an expert, you have something that attracted the employer. If you do not calm down completely, try not to show it.

Stay loose and relaxed. Do not try to act out the play and pretend to be superhuman.

And if you are dealing with an experienced interviewer he easily fills the trap and you will solve your game.
Stay open and friendly, do not forget to smile (but do not do it constantly).

Responding to a question
Remember the interviewer is more interested how you respond.

After all, interviews are more aimed at clarifying not professional and personal qualities of the candidate, his communication skills, ability to articulate, self-confidence, stress, etc.

Your language should be concise and clear, it is not necessary to go into unnecessary details.

When answering the questions better look the interviewer in the eye and avoid unnecessary gestures.

*** Be able to withstand a pause.
If you've answered the question, and the interviewer is still silent, it is not necessary to make any further comments. Wait for him to speak first.

When it's over, do not forget to smile and ask about how you did in the interview.

If you are denied work, do not despair.

First of all, you will be offered job even better and you will get it.

Second, you have acquired a unique experience of survival in extreme conditions, which is sure to come in handy in the future job search.

Passing the interview is also a skill that is necessary to be able to master.

Therefore, having calmed down, try to analyze entire interview and understand what mistakes were made in order to avoid them in the future.

Popular Questions Managers Will ask?

1) What are your disadvantages?
2) Why are gone from your former place of work?
3) How long do you want to work with us here?
4) Why do you want to work with us?
5) At what salary you are applying for?
6) Why is blue curacao blue? (Great question)
7) Why is gin Bombay Sapphire blue? (Great question)

Good Answers?

1) Neutral response, I have, of course, disadvantages, but they have no effect on my work.

2) It is not anticipated career

3) I have to work a little and see if the team likes to be close to me in a team atmosphere. If all you like, then our cooperation will be long and mutually beneficial

4) Interesting place, excellent service, convenient location.

5) Feel free to call the amount that is 10-15% higher than the previous salary.
   Maximum – 30%

6) Because it contains food coloring

7) Because the blue bottle, gin clear!

They Hire You. Now What?
Things to do/Ask before your first shift?
Try to find out as much information about a bar in which you will work.
How to store inventory, where are stored the extra tools, how work in this bar, etc.

What are The Best Ways to Ask For/Get a Raise, Promotion & Better Shifts?
To keep up to show results. Put yourself in the shoes of your boss and think about what you want to see. You need to systematically show the result, for example if you are a bartender it is: a good and stable selling drinks more than their colleagues

You create a fun atmosphere at the bar doing such flair show at the bar

You attract a large number of guests

You are a business card of bar!

You train your colleagues!

All this may be the reason for your promotion.

Talk to your boss and compare the facts as it was before you and how to become a better you!

Ryan Millar
In the bar, hospitality and flair industry for 14 years. Instructor and Trainer with

ExtremeBartending.com for 13 years.

Traveled all around North America and Internationally teaching and performing flair shows including numerous private parties (example: Charles Simonyi, inventor of Microsoft Word, Excel and The Playboy Mansion)

Ryan Says:
What Increases The Odds Of A Bartender Getting Hired?
To increase your odds of getting hired at your preferred bar you need to stick out in the crowd. You can only imagine how many resumes mangers get a day.

Showcase that you are a social person:
Have a gathering or party at this bar.
Bring down about 30+ people. This will show the manager that you are more the just a bartender but some that can add to packing out their bar.

Simple math: More people = More Money for the bar = Happy Owner/Management.
Then bring up the party to the manager and thank them for having them at their bar.

How to Choose Which Bars To Apply At?

I always looked for places that I would want to hang out at if I didn't work there not to mention a place where I can invite my friends to.

This is going to be your home.
If you like where you are, people will see this in you and be more likely to come there, stay longer, spend more money etc..

Also look for places that you can see yourself wanting to add value to making it even that much better.

A major deciding factor is the staff and management.
Are they excited about they do?
Do people like coming to work?
This is your chance to ask questions of the people who are working.

Bottom line:

The more you love where you are and what you do the more money you will make!

 **Clint Pitts** – 16 years in the industry. My strengths that have resulted in a successful career include leading and motivating people, training and developing both hourly employees and managers.

Clint Says:
The Best Ways to Ask For/Get a Raise, Promotion & Better Shifts?
Do great work. Then remember if you don't ask you don't get.

By proving yourself, that your worth better shifts, that you have created a solid clientele Prove yourself first

 **Dawn Ottier** - Hi Scott, What can I say, I started in the industry over 14 years ago at the age of 22 working in a pub and have worn many hats simultaneously in the industry.

I have served, bartended and quickly become part of the administrative side as well. That's the beauty of this industry, your talents are found, recognized and brought into play. Through the many years, the bonds and friendships made along the way, the ever changing fads and mixology and styles, the one constant always remains. The value of your customers!

Thanks for including me in such a vast and experienced group!! I enjoyed answering some of those questions. Looks as though you've been a part of another great creation Scott.

Dawn Says:
What are The Best Ways to Ask For/Get a Raise,
Promotion & Better Shifts?
Did you have a letter with you describing what you wanted
and why you deserve it?
This is a great question!

Firstly, your manager and/or management team are there
to support you, to encourage growth within the company.

Having a valuable employee who is eager to learn and
advance is an asset to the company and a great manager
can and will recognize that.
Having said that, part of the growth and advancement
within a company is knowing your value and going for it.

If there is a specific position you are looking to advance to,
researching what the qualifications are, what the position
involves and preparing yourself for that.

Writing out a plan with this information shows initiative
and forethought.

Be able to show how this raise or advancement can help
the revenue of the company.

Make an appointment with your boss to have this
discussion is a good idea and make sure it's a time when
your manager or boss has time.

Meaning your boss has deadlines and financial dealings
regarding the company to handle on a regular basis.

Making sure to speak to him/her/them at a time when they can see the benefit of this.

Shaun Daugherty – I have over twenty years' experience in the bar and restaurant industry, with most of that time as a bartender, bar manager, consultant.
Author of "Extra Dry with a Twist: An Insider's Guide to Bartending". www. shaunthebartender.com

Shaun Says:
Best Ways to Ask For/Get a Raise, Promotion & Better Shifts?
In my opinion, getting a raise, a promotion and better shifts depends on how well you do behind the bar.

Also, if you need to ask for a raise to receive one as a bartender, you are in the wrong occupation.

We as bartenders give ourselves raises by attracting more customers in and receiving more in tips.

Having to ask for more money should only happen if you are training other bartenders, or you are doing more than what you were originally expecting, like inventory for your managers, placing orders, etc.

Another reason would be that you have built up your customer base and they have decided to bring another bartender in to help out.

The bar better be ready for you to ask for compensation since you now have lost half your tips due to bringing someone else in.

When to ask?
Only when you are a Senior Bartender or a Trainer is when you should ask for a raise.

What to ask?
"Since my responsibilities seem to exceed what my job description is, what type of compensation can I expect?"

How often to ask?
If you have to ask for a raise more than once, you may want to start looking for something else if you feel you deserve it.

What increases your odds?
You have to be at the top of your game to expect to bar to compensate you or feel they have to. Make the job, while you are there, the number one priority.

Did you have a plan?
I have never asked for a raise, because I have never had to. If you do, you better have a game plan and good timing.

Did you have a letter with you describing what you wanted and why you deserve it?
This, of course, would go along with having a plan.

You should put bullet points together on why you feel you deserve a raise and the things you do to make these feelings factual.

If you're a manager, what advice can you give to employees?

Be a professional and work had and honestly so you can give yourself a raise by bringing in more customers.

The greatest thing about tending bar is that it is up to you to decide when you get a raise by getting more people to frequent your establishment.

We all understand that the tips are what we are most dependent on, so to get a raise maybe you should up your game.

Entertain all who enter your establishment, make sure no one waits too long for the next round, introduce customers to one another so they feel they belong, etc.

We are the controllers of our own fate in this business.

If you do your job well, a raise, be it in regards to hourly or from just being awesome and making more tips, will be what you get on a frequent basis.

 **Kristy Koehler** – 12 years in the industry. Started serving at 18, bartending at 19 as a way to get through University, but fell in love with the industry and decided to pursue it instead of a career in law. Has been bartending for 7 years, owned a bartending school, and became incredibly passionate about the wine aspect of the industry.

Is now a Sommelier and Wine Consultant, with certifications from the Sake Education Council of Japan, Wine and Spirit Education Trust, Court of Master Sommeliers, and the the Wine Academy of Spain.

Kristy Says:
Resumes
5 Big Mistakes to avoid

1. Don't use text language (i.e. UR instead of your)

2. Make sure your e-mail address is professional. i.e. bobsmith@blahblah.com, not <u>sexypotsmokingskank@ blahblah.com</u>

3. Don't use the standard high school format (i.e. OBJECTIVE: To gain permanent part-time or full-time employment in a professional atmosphzzzz.......)

Examples/Stories of Great Resumes?
A guy with no bartending experience related every single one of his jobs to how it would help him in his new chosen career.

For example:
He said that working the late night stocking shift at Home Depot had prepared him for late nights. Working the counter at Subway had helped him with cash handling and dealing with customers who are in a hurry and who might want modified ingredients.

He also listed three fun facts about himself like what a great magician he was and how he had been to the pyramids.

It made me feel connected with him before I even brought him in for the interview.

Examples/Stories of Terrible Resumes
Someone's e-mail address, listed in bold on the top of the resume went a little something like this i.grab.my.nutsack@blahblah.com

Making a great cover letter?
Address is to the name of the manager
I only ever had two people call ahead to find out my name and I hired both of them!

Do not address your cover letter to
"To Whom It May Concern"
or
"Dear Sir/Madame"

PERSONALIZE IT!!

What are The Best Ways to Ask For/Get a Raise, Promotion & Better Shifts?
When to ask?
Not in the middle of dinner service!
Come in on a day off, before the shift starts - and not on a busy day.

Make an appointment with the boss – don't just drop in and surprise him.

How often to ask?

Once – If he flat out says no without offering ways to improve your chances next time, move on.

What increases your odds?

Being a good worker – having the proper information to back up your claims of being a good worker (i.e. the last four times you called me to come in early I said yes)

How do you bring it up?

Send him an e-mail or note asking to meet to discuss your advancement opportunities.

If you're a manager, what advice can you give to employees?

Don't tell me what a good worker you are if you can't back it up!

I need examples, dates, etc. to show me that you've been thinking this through and aren't just some entitled hot shot.

Cite customer comment cards, bartending knowledge, etc.

 **Eddy Kalman** – Head bartender in Quids Inn in Coventry, UK, but I also work as a part time bartender in Club Heat. I started working in bars when I was 16 as a piccolo - glass collector, bartender's little helper - because in Romania you are not legally allowed to work when you're that young. When I turned 18 I had my first bartender job and I loved it! The

drinks, the girls, the happiness on people's faces, their expressions when they drink the concoction you just made for them... seeing an occasional bar fight - but hey, there has to be a downside!

Eddy Says:
What are The Best Ways to Ask For/Get a Raise, Promotion & Better Shifts?
Well if you have an ask, I think the first thing to do is ask yourself whether you deserve it or not.

Why would you deserve it and not your colleague?

From my experience if you work harder than everyone else your manager should see it and a good manager would know that you're the one that needs promoted when a better position is available.

I never had to ask for a raise, my wage increased from time to time because my manager noticed that I make her job easier.

I believe that proving that you deserve a raise works better than asking for a raise. Whenever we have no one to serve I make myself useful and that's how I got noticed.

I spot things that need fixing that my manager didn't, help out with the stock, calculate other bar staff hours / wages.

Move things around to serve faster, ask the manager to buy stuff needed in the bar – whenever she didn't buy then, I bought it myself and proved her that they're useful.

When I got employed at this bar there was no such position of Head Bartender. I asked for it myself, but it came with a lot more responsibilities.

Ways to prove yourself:
Multitask while you're serving, punctuality (no one can rely on a bartender that doesn't come on time), no unnecessary brakes, when you're needed give 200%, be trustworthy.

Whenever my boss (the owner) comes for a drink I keep an extra eye on him.
He's not only a customer, he pays my wages. I always make sure that he has everything that he needs and I even do table service for him.

I'm my manager's right hand in the bar and I hear all the stories about asking for raises and better shifts:

Best story:
I started working on a 4.75 hourly wage and now I get 7.5 after three years of working in the bar and this year I also got a work car (Vauxhall Astrovan bought by the bar, I don't pay insurance for it, Road Tax, repairs etc.).

One of my colleagues that got employed one year after me he started with 5 pounds an hour and about three months ago he thought that he should ask for a raise.

He printed a letter that said the following:
'Dear Irina, I have been working here for the past two years and I was wondering if you can increase my wage. I am

not doing amazing financially and a raise would be very welcome. Hope you will consider it. Thank you in advance, Sonny.'

The guy is working very slow, he's never smiling, he's always asking to go home earlier, he's sometimes late to work and about 5-6 times a year he doesn't wake up to come to work.
After she told me that he asked for a raise, she wanted my opinion:
I told her that she should fire him, not to give him a raise.

Now the way that she played it is kind of admirable (in my opinion):
She had a 1-on-1 meeting with him and she told him that he got a raise from 5 to 5.75, because he's been with us for two years, but he needs to get his standards up and maybe in the future he'll get another raise.

The guy improved for the first two weeks, but he went back to his normal state after that. Eventually he got fired one month after his downfall.

Dan Bangay-Hi Scott, I have been in the industry for about 20 years now, since I was 18. I started in Melbourne.

· I started as a bussie and worked for two years at various clubs
· Worked as a bartender and learnt flair for the next six years

· Did security for two years in over 20 bars
· Started my leadership development and management skills over the last nine years

What Increases The Odds Of A Bartender Getting Hired?
I always look for passion, I can teach anything except passion and enthusiasm.

How to Choose Which Bars To Apply At?
If I need money I look for the busiest
If I need a career I look for part of a bar that's part of a chain
If I want fun I look for a young crowd

Resumes
As a bartender I was always poached so I never had to have a resume, as a manager
I look for brief and easy to read, and personal touches stick out especially humour in hospitality.

Things to include
A photo, previous experience, personal goals, your contact details, availability

Big Mistakes to avoid
Too much detail, non-relevant issues, non-relevant experience,

What were some of the challenges you faced getting a Bartending job
Getting bar experience as a busser

The Interview
What advice do you have for bartenders?
Be honest, don't waste our time if we are going to fire
you in a week for bullshitting during the interview

Popular Questions Managers will ask?
Where have you worked, why did you quit, what do you
want from this job

Good Answers?
Various bars around the world, wanted to move upward/
stopped learning, to develop my skills and learn more

Good Questions to ask them?
Product knowledge and venue knowledge questions

They Hire You. Now What?
Things to do/Ask before your first shift?
Price list, house specials,
cocktail list, SOPs (Standard Operating Procedures)
Your First Shift. Suggestions on how to do great?
Deliver great service, display great product knowledge,
make plenty of sales.

**What are The Best Ways to Ask For/Get a Raise,
Promotion & Better Shifts?**
Be the best employee and show you are worth the raise,
step up a notch and give examples of why you are worth it

When to ask?
When the boss is happy and before a busy part of the year

What to ask?
Be straight forward and to the point but don't be forceful or demanding

How often to ask?
Once a year

What increases your odds?
Be an exemplary employee

How do you bring it up?
Ask the boss if you can have five minutes of his time to discuss your progression

Brian Rypien
I've been in the hospitality industry for a total of around 17 years, bartended at the Roxy for eight years (with Scott Young), bartended at the Hyatt regency hotel in the Cayman Islands for two years, worked at The Keg for two years, worked at the Spaghetti Factory for a couple of years, bartended and waitered at the Pan Pacific Hotel for three years and am currently bartending / watering (two years) at the Pinnacle on the Pier Hotel in North Vancouver.

Back in the Caymans now

What Increases The Odds Of A Bartender Getting Hired?

Hate to say it but age plays a key role with getting hired (youth and enthusiasm) and then experience. Personality comes in third.

How to Choose Which Bars To Apply At?

I'd say start with restaurants, then Hotels and get enough on your resume to get a good shot at a busy night club is you so desire

How to Create a Great Resume?

Get professional help to put together a good solid resume, costs are minimal and worth it.

Making a great cover letter?

Making a great cover letter is HUGE, that's why I recommend a professional to do it.

I got hired over the phone when I got the gig in the Cayman Islands.
I put in the letter how I had served famous people like the Royal Couple and it instantly impressed him, but you have to do it with tact.

The Interview – What advice do you have for bartenders?

Just be yourself, don't try too hard, come off as humble but personable

What were some of the challenges you faced getting a Bartending job?

Some of the challenges are getting a chance, a lot of times it's who you know, don't be afraid to take a lower position.

I started out as a Door man at the Roxy And then a bar back, I did this with a boat load of experience. Started out as a busser at The Keg.
You just need to get your foot in the door

What was your worst interviewing experience?
I was told to tell a joke……. I'm a pretty funny guy but I froze….told a terrible joke…
but did get the job anyways.

What was your best interviewing experience?
Best was when I was interviewing for the Pan Pacific and had to go through five interviews, the manager, head chef, F&B manager…..
passed with a little blood, sweat and tears.

What to do/bring/say?
Be precise with your answers, bring your personality, say what comes naturally……
be your self

What not to do/bring/say in an interview?
Do not carry on about yourself (no bragging).
Talk about how you are with people but reserve to pat yourself on the back.

Popular Questions Managers Will ask?
How are you with the public? How are you with other employees?
How would you be an asset to this company?

Good Answers?

I am very good with people (good people skills),
I get along very well with other employees,
I really enjoy the hospitality industry for those reasons,

They Hire You. Now What?
10 Things to do/Ask before your first shift?

Learn the menu! What kind of drinks will be served, be ready to take on whatever they throw at you. Just be prepared for what kind of place you'll be working at and you'll impress right off the bat.

Your First Shift. Suggestions on how to do great?

Don't be cocky! If you need help, humble yourself and ask for it.
Fellow employees will accept you a lot quicker if you are human and not a dick.

Matt Hamilton
I've worked in the service industry for 14 years. First started back of the house but made the switch once I realized where the real money was.
I have bartended in a variety of places from restaurants to lounges to nightclubs.

Matt Says:
What Increases The Odds Of A Bartender Getting Hired?
Experience is the one thing that stands out. If you have experience on your resume, worked at recognizable establishments, it will go a long way.

Also if you've had training, in the art of making a cocktail, semolina, etc. that will make you stand out from the rest.

How to Choose Which Bars To Apply At?
It depends what you're looking for. Ideally you'd want to a place that's high volume but also somewhere that you'll be happy to work at.

If elaborate cocktails frustrate you, you might be better off going to a pub or a nightclub where you'd primarily be making highballs and opening bottles of beer.

If you take pride in making labour-intensive cocktail, look into some trendy lounge's or restaurants.

How to Create a Great Resume?
Have a cover letter that represents who you are and what your goals are.

It does you no service just to blow smoke because in the end, you're entering in a partnership with your job and you guys both have to make the best of it.

Things to include Include
Your education – having someone with a completed degree says a lot about your character, you're willing to dedicate yourself and push yourself for four years.

Your work history, even if it doesn't include restaurants. It will say a lot about you.

All your contact information should be in the header, name, address, phone, e-mail. Make it easy for them to contact you. The name should be in bigger font so it sticks out.

It's helpful to include a HOBBIES section, really says who you are outside of work.

5 Big Mistakes to avoid
Nothing too wordy. Don't describe every responsibility you had as a bartender at a previous place, it's redundant and your prospective employer will understand.

Keep it one page. The page should look easy to read so take advantage of white space and make it neat. And never lie, it's not worth it.

Examples/Stories of Terrible Resumes
Repetitive information, multiple bars and a paragraph of the responsibilities under each. It looked and read terribly.

Making a great cover letter?
A great cover letter should say what your goal is, illustrate your strengths and your prospective employer should get a sense of who you are and why they should hire you.

What were some of the challenges you faced getting a Bartending job

Lack of experience. Sometimes if you don't have experience, you'll have to work your way up. While it doesn't seem ideal, it shows your prospective employer that you're willing to work to get where you're at.

The Interview - What advice do you have for bartenders?

Just relax, be yourself but be confident. Don't be nervous, think of this as a great opportunity. If the owner/manager is interviewer you, they want to hire you.
They need an employee so use that to your advantage.

What to do/bring/say?

You should look sharp, nothing over the top but dress to impress.
Bring another resume and cover letter, just in case.

Popular Questions Managers Will ask?

Why should I hire you, have you ever worked in a place like this before

Good Answers?

Have answers for those questions ready. Be prepared to sell yourself.

Good Questions to ask them?

It is always a good thing to ask questions, shows you're interested.

What sets this place apart from the numerous other places around?

What kind of staff incentive programs are there?

Is there a minimum shift requirement?

What kind of hours does the place keep?

They Hire You. Now What?

10 Things to do/Ask before your first shift?
Show up early.
Always ask if there is anything else you can do.
Be eager, ask questions. And remember, there is never a stupid question.

Come prepared, have pens, pads etc.

Make sure your in proper uniform and it is clean.
Make sure your groomed according to restaurant specifications.

Your First Shift. Suggestions on how to do great?
Never be afraid to do more.
Set the bar high, ask what else you can help with.

Take notes.
You're the new guy so you'll be the outsider but a good way to be accepted by the staff is to introduce yourself and be friendly.

Rob Turek – President of the Cleveland Chapter of the United States Bartender's Guild.

Born in July of 1971, yet appearing much younger than his birthdate shows, Rob Turek began his bartending career in the summer of 1996.

Sitting on a stool at Cleveland's Professional Bartending School (Yes, bartending school…. he actually attended one), a dream began to form within him to become the best bartender possible.

It was a page from the school textbook entitled "about the author," where Rob discovered the existence of world bartender competitions, most notably Walt Disney Resorts' Quest for the Best Bartender in the World!

He has worked in some of the top establishments in Cleveland from BAR Cleveland and Banana Joe's in the Flats, to the trendy lounges such as Wish and Spy Bar, to name a few.

Fifteen years later, and a plethora of awards, Rob was named the Best Cleveland Bartender by The Cleveland Plain Dealer and Cleveland.com! Driven to succeed, Rob will never compromise his quest for excellence in becoming the best bartender Cleveland has ever seen.

Here are a few things about Rob Turek you may not know…
- Rob was featured on the National TV Show "Dr. Oz".
- A Co-Chairman of the United States Bartender Guild National Flair Council

And he recently placed third in America in the Absolut Best Bloody Mary competition hosted by Food Network's Chopped Show.
Rob is currently bartending at the Barley House in Cleveland, the city's hottest nightspot.

Rob Says:
What Increases The Odds Of A Bartender Getting Hired?
In my opinion, PASSION.

Passion is a contagious personality trait that attracts others. Bar owners will notice if one is passionate.

Obviously, factors such as experience, training, etc., are prerequisites, but passion and desire to work hard can overcome a lack of experience and/or training.

Preparation and work study is also a key to success. Get good at the craft, and go after your dream job passionately.

How to Choose Which Bars To Apply At?
Choose the bar that best fits your personality.

If you're an avid golfer, you may want to consider working at a Country Club.
If you want to make fast money and not have to chat it up much with guests, then apply at high volume nightclubs.
If you're big on getting to know your guests, then perhaps the neighbourhood joint is the one for you.

Also, do a little recon before applying somewhere.
Stop in a few times, and see how the service is, how busy it is, etc.
If the place is busy and service is great, then chances are the place has strong management and good systems.

You want to work in a place that will set you up for success.

How to Create a Great Resume?
I myself like fun resumes, that are short and sweet.

Employers are going to take a quick glance, but it is your chance to show who you are as a personality on paper.

Don't overdo it with every job you've ever had.
Give them enough to see that you qualify.
This is another way to show your passion for the craft.

5 Things to include?
Any background that is pertinent to the job.
You are in the business of hospitality.
Point out past employers and a few bullet points of the good things you did to help that particular establishments success.

Examples/Stories of great Resumes?
Cheryl Charming has some fun resume templates. http://www.misscharming.com/
I believe with today's technology, a video resume would be awesome!

What advice do you have for bartenders?
Dress the part similar to the work uniform. This will allow the interviewer to picture you as an employee. Be well kept, and clean, and don't be afraid to show your personality.

What were some of the challenges you faced getting a Bartending job?
I went to bartending school, and that provided a challenge for me, as most graduates think that bartending school is strong enough to get hired.

However, most managers came up through the "school of hard knocks" within the line of promotion. They want people with experience. It took some time for me to gain more and more experience and a reputation to where employers started to want me, rather than me "want them".

What was your worst interviewing experience?
I once interviewed with Bahama Breeze, and they incorporated flair into their bar. Throughout the interview, however, the interviewer didn't take my resume serious, and when I wanted to show him what I could do, he said he didn't have time.

He dropped the ball with that one.
Why even interview me in the first place??? He wasn't there shortly thereafter…

What was your best interviewing experience?
When I interviewed with Kalahari Resorts. They were looking for flair bartenders for their Sandusky resort Kahunaville. I had a strong flair team in place called "STARTENDERS". I went into the interview with my team of 5 guys, and blew them away! They instantly hired all of us at once!

What to do/bring/say?
Show your personality. Be the person you are behind the stick. And smile.
This is one thing most interviewers will look for, so show your pearly whites!
Also if you haven't applied yet, bring your own pen.

What not to do/bring/say in an interview?
Don't be too demanding. You are applying for a job with them, they aren't applying to be with you. Don't bad talk any previous jobs. That can come back to bite you….

Popular Questions Managers Will ask?
Why should we hire you? What makes you qualified for the position?
What experience do you have? Are you a team player?

Good Answers?
Because I believe I have the skills, that together with your work systems, I could be an asset for your establishment.

I have the personality type that works well socially with others.

I have the ability to multi-task and think quick on my feet, not to mention, my irresistible smile! I have experience working …… and I have a training background of which includes…..
I believe that a great team behind the bar is the key for successful service.
I work well with co-workers and offer leadership when needed, particularly during stressful moments.

Good Questions to ask them?
Is there anything specific I should know as far as your policies?
What is the main goal and focus of your establishment?

Your First Shift. Suggestions on how to do great?
Always come prepared.

Come as a professional bartender with two or three working pens, a wine key, bottle opener, neatly groomed, clean nails, etc.

Find the bartender with the most repertoire and professionalism and watch them.

Ken Lam – Flair Iron Bartending Education Entertainment Co. Ltd. / WFA World Flair Association (Hong Kong)

I am from Hong Kong. I learned Flair around five years ago. I have my Flair team in Hong Kong called Fair Iron. Our target is promoting flair culture and cocktail mixology skills in Hong Kong.

What were some of the challenges you faced getting a Bartending job?
You need to know what the main trend is of the food and beverage market.

Usually it's wine in Hong Kong, so that's why so many restaurants are focused on sommeliers more than bartenders. But you should show what you can do, or what you can change or areas you're working on.

Also, create some great cocktail to increase the sales, and using flair can provide more entertainment for the bar or restaurant.

It's Your First Shift. Suggestions on how to do great?
Just learn from your colleagues and try to build up good communication with all of them.
Even though you may have great experience, you should remember you are new there.

Cathy Love
Cathy (in red) Scotty in front.
I worked in the industry for 15 years. Most of my experience was as a waitress, but also worked in the kitchen and as a hostess. My favourite of all of my experiences was working at the Roxy in Vancouver, where I met Scotty, and everyone else with whom I loved working.

Working in the service industry taught me the importance of being part of a team, helped to develop confidence, and how to manage time when it got crazy busy.

You learned pretty quickly not only what your regulars drank, but also the non-regulars, making it easier to take orders from across the room with just a glance.

Cathy Says:
What Increases The Odds Of A Bartender Getting Hired?
I would say probably skills, knowledge, ability, and a great personality.
With a great personality and S/K/A comes additional friends/customers/regulars.

How to Choose Which Bars To Apply At?
Choose bars that are well-established, but still busy and progressive in their ideas/marketing. Having said that, new bars that fill a specific niche can be incredibly profitable

and bring in a higher-paying clientele, which would be very beneficial to the bartender.

I also think that you need to look at staff turn-over.
The higher the staff turn-over, the greater risk of internal problems,
i.e. managerial issues.

How to Create a Great Resume?
In my experience, the best resumes are short and to the point.

While some people say that one page is the absolute maximum, these days I believe it's acceptable to stretch it to two pages – and ensure your name and personal information is at the top of both pages.

You don't want to have a page go missing. Use bullet points to describe experiences, educational background, etc. And keep your Work Experiences relevant to the job you're looking for – you don't need to include what you did flipping burgers in 1979.

Start with the most recent Work Experience and work backwards.

I've never been a fan of the "Objectives" section on standard resumes – everybody knows you're looking for a job at their establishment. It's redundant.
In my experience, people are more interested in your qualifications and experience.

PROOFREAD IT!!!!! While a typo or five in a resume doesn't necessarily ensure that it will go straight into the shredder, it just doesn't look good. Ask someone else to look it over to make sure it's all correct.

Use good paper and a good printer.

Most importantly, bear in mind that the top half of the first page will usually either grab their interest, or it won't. So make sure your top job experiences or two have the most interesting information.

5 Things to include
Keep in mind the use of certain keywords, and be specific to the industry/establishment where you're hoping to gain work.

Use action words as well, such as: coached, managed, planned…

Again, make sure you include your full name and contact information on the top of every page Include volunteer information as part of your work experience, or in a "summary" portion at the bottom.

This is important to potential employers because it is part of your "experiences".
Awards or special recognitions should be included.

5 Big Mistakes to avoid
Don't go into the interview process with NO idea of what the company/establishment does. Have some basic

knowledge of its successes. Make sure you keep personal details off your resume – i.e. marital status, race, age, etc.

Making a great cover letter?
Every cover letter should be customized to go with each resume sent out – not just a mass, generic letter. Do some research into the company where you're seeking employment.

Include keywords relevant to that establishment, and to the position you're applying for.
Remember to sell yourself, keep it upbeat and outline what you can offer to the establishment.

The cover letter should basically sum up the resume in about a half a page – it doesn't need to be long and detailed – and it asks for the job.

According to Forbes Magazine, some of their key items for a successful cover letter are:

- Don't repeat your resume

- Address nobody (not even "to whom it may concern")

  Just jump right into something juicy

- Never use "My name is [whatever], and I am applying for

  the position of [whatever]." They already know this; and

  finally, close QUICKLY and strong.

The Interview
What advice do you have for bartenders?
Bring your A-personality to the interview. You want to be 'on' but not obnoxious.
Be friendly, confident.

What to do/bring/say?
If you tell them you're flexible, MEAN IT.
Be available when you say you will be.
Don't just tell them what you think they want to hear.

What not to do/bring/say in an interview?
Don't be late!!!
Don't ask how much the pay is.
Don't cut down previous employers or places of employment.

If asked for your shortcomings, don't say you're not aware of any – everybody has them.

And when they ask you if you have any questions for them, come prepared with one or two. It shows your interest.

Good Questions to ask them?
What brought you to this company?
What do you enjoy most about working here?
Ask questions of the "get to know the company" variety.

What are The Best Ways to Ask For/Get a Raise, Promotion & Better Shifts?

Ask for a raise – don't beg for it. Don't tell them you're having money problems or some other big sob story. You need to make it clear that you DESERVE it.

Show your boss that you will continue to try to improve yourself and your work so that the company will benefit for years to come – show your commitment.

If you make yourself an invaluable part of the company, you'll gain more leverage in asking for a raise. If you can show that you're responsible for huge increases or possess knowledge that is irreplaceable, they may be more open to paying you more to keep you.

Try to pick a time when you expect your boss to be in a better mood.

PRACTICE what you're going to say – be prepared.

Have someone quiz you and come up with possible answers to possible questions.

 **Mariana Berdainu** - http://instagram.com/mbeyeline21
3 years in this industry as a whole
6 different jobs
passion: music

Mariana Says:
Why/how you got into the industry?
Got into bartending by choice. It was my first year in the states and I needed to support myself and I thought: out of all people I met so far, who is surrounded by music, makes nice money and is content with their jobs?

Bartenders. But the difference between me and my friends is that from the very beginning I had my eyes set on big establishments where you make top dollars.

So it was never an issue for me getting out of my comfort zone and quitting a good job for an even better one. Chasing the money got me the needed experience.

After interviewing with top upscale establishments in NYC (and we're talking high end restaurants, clubs, strip clubs, lounges), I've seen a pattern in what employers like to ask potential bartenders.

2- How did you become a bartender?
Everyone has a story about this. I was invited to a club party and I was lost.
I couldn't find the address and it was my 2nd week in the States. I was only 18 at the time. So I told myself I'll ask the first person I see if they know where the address is. Which I did.

Surprisingly the guy was the head bartender of the club, which I later on discovered it was one of the top preferred celebrity spots in NYC.

I kept hanging out with the bartender and he introduced me to the manager. We all became friends and I wasn't thinking of bartending at the time, but I noticed that out of all people I met, him, the bartender, was the richest, happiest and most well connected person too. And about a year later when I was in a financial crisis, I was like: oh well, time to bartend.

3- What Increases The Odds Of A Bartender Getting Hired?

1. **Stellar Resume**
   (think of it like this: if you wanna stand out, you have to be outstanding).

   When you walk in with a resume that looks like the pile of resumes that the manager already has on his desk and never took a second look at it, well that's where your potential will end up: in the pile.

2. **Looks.**
   From hairstyle to fingernails and shoes.
   This is not me being vain, it is the truth.

3. **Smiling during the interview.**
   Put the employer at ease and make them feel comfortable around you.

4. **Telling them what they wanna hear.**
   You have to. Not my rules.

5. **Having a self-confident attitude without coming off as stuck up.**
They want a leader behind the bar after all.

6. **Following up.**
It does make a difference.

If you have 5 resumes on the table and all of them are equally qualified, who will you hire? The 4 ones that never followed up or the 5th that called you two times about the job and really wants it?

4- How to Choose Which Bars To Apply At?
You choose based off your personality and where you fit best, where you feel you can thrive. I tried clubs, nightclubs, lounges, restaurants, sports bars and I know for a fact I am not made for restaurants or steakhouses.

Give me a bar. A real bar. A place where people come to drink first and all else second.

I refuse to work in a setting where I do service bar only or I have to serve as much food as cocktails. But that's just me. Other bartenders quite enjoy the steady flow of restaurants and lounges. I want people. And lots of them ordering DRINKS at the same time!

5- How to Create a Great Resume?
By focusing on your key qualifications and targeting the type of establishments you're pursuing.

If you want to be hired in a club, you need an upbeat beautiful and fancy resume template with references that focus on how fast you are and what are your top sales records.

On the other side, if you are looking to bartend in a fine dining restaurant you will need a very serious vibe on your resume, corporate-like key pointers and very official language and bartending terms.

I always include in my resumes:

1. POS systems I am proficient in
2. The fact that I am fluent in 4 languages
3. I mention work-related certificates and awards
   (like TIPS certificate, NY state license etc)
4. Brief personality description
5. HD photo on the front page of my resume

These are my must 5 to include,
but let's not forget the basics like work history and education.

7- Big Mistakes to avoid

1. Never blame your former manager, establishment, coworkers as the reason for leaving. Your actual employer will be thinking that you'll say the exact same thing about them too when you leave, because we all leave sooner or later.

You'll never work forever in a place.

But the reputation that leaves with you matters to any manager/owner.

2. Forget about the volunteer work and all small jobs you did in high school and college. No one cares. You're going to sell alcohol. These people wanna know that you understand your duties and responsibilities.

   Trying to look like Mother Theresa on your resume won't help you with anything.

3. **Never accept a beverage from any employer during an interview.**
   It's a TRAP!

   They wanna see your weakness for alcohol and also if you know etiquette of respecting people's time. He is not there to make drinks for you. He is there to interview you. Don't shoot yourself in the foot before you even get a chance to show your skills behind the bar.

4. **A big mistake is not asking about barbacks and tip outs from the start.**
   Some bartenders will tell you otherwise and that it is actually better staying away from money discussions in the beginning.

   But time is money and I don't wanna train for a week and invest the time to later find out that there is no barback and if there is one the tip out percentage is outrageous. That matters to me.

5. **Not thanking people for their time.**
   In a world that's so rude and so cold, being nice makes
   a difference.
   Thank people for seeing you, interviewing you and for
   their time altogether.

8- Examples/Stories of great Resumes?
I always get complimented on my resumes.
To the point that the managers will pass it on to each other
and stare in awe at it.

My resume is made of 8 pages.

The 1st cover page is color printed and for half of the paper
is my photo with the contact info right under, on the rest
of the page are my key qualifications.

2nd page is my work history, work accomplishments and
education.

3rd page is a color copy of my Bartender license,
4th page is a color copy of my wine service certificate,
5th page is a copy of my TIPS certificate,
6th up to the 8th are references from former employers.

So yes, you make an impression when you go in with an 8
pages color resume.

That lets them know you took the time, effort and money
to put it together.

It's just mind blowing to them to see something so stellar compared to the black and white one page regular resumes they get on a daily basis.

9- Examples/Stories of Terrible Resumes
My husband manages a fine dining restaurant in Harlem and often he'll bring home resumes for us to take a look together and help him decide who to hire.

I remember this resume, it didn't even make sense! The wording was incoherent and it sounded like it was copy/pasted from google translator.

It turned out the person didn't even know english. It became the barometer for a bad resume in our house.

10- Making a great cover letter?
I don't do those. Like I said above, photo, contact info and key qualifications on the front page speak for themselves in my opinion. It has worked for me so far.

11 - What were some of the challenges you faced getting a Bartending job?
Being discriminated against.
There have been occasions when I knew for a fact I was better than all of the bartenders working in that establishment and the most qualified, but because I didn't fit in a certain preferred race, I was never given the chance to even prove myself.

And you know, I've learned to tell those racist employers right away. Since I am from Eastern Europe, I have a slight accent and instead of saying 'so for how long you've been bartending' and all work related questions, they'll ask you where are you from, when did you come to the States and how old are you.

Rude, impolite and not worth my time (or YOURS!).

I've paid my dues to become a resident and I deserve to be treated based off my skills and qualifications, not my nationality.

They Hire You. Now What?
20- 10 Things to do/Ask before your first shift?

1. **Check in with the dress code.** Every bar is different.

2. **Check in with the tools you need to have on you.**
   I was once asked to bring a knife because they don't provide one for cutting fruits (of course I never went back).

3. **Get the manager's phone number/e-mail address.**
   Anything can happen from today until tomorrow.

   In case something does happen and you can't make it to the training, you need a phone number to call and inform the manager on your situation.

4. **Learn the specialty cocktails in advance.**
   It will ease your first shifts so much!
   And will make your new coworkers respect you because you're learning and studying on your own!

5. **Try to learn as much as possible about the bartender who'll train you.**
   The more you can guess their personalities in advance, the easier it will be to get on their good side.

6. **Get a mental list with questions you need to know** to feel comfortable behind the bar and ask them on the go!

7. **Ask what are the no tolerance rules and laws.**
   I remember once I wasn't told in advance that I can't ask for anyone's help so I got the help of a server to cut a pineapple, and when the manager saw it he warned me that if ever repeated, I'll get fired because by distracting coworkers to help me I distract the whole flow of the business.

8. **Ask when exactly are you expected to be ready to work.**
   If they tell you 5 pm, you better be there at 4:30.

9. **Get some snacks in your bag.**
   I never liked taking breaks or excuse myself to eat on my first shift, not even in my first months!
   But... Some shifts are super long and if you're like me, you'll have peanuts or protein bars in your bag and snack some when and where no one can see you.

10. **Sleep well!**
    Go to sleep early because most likely you will be nervous and will need some time to fall asleep and last thing you want on your first day is to be obviously tired.

If you work for a cruise line or resort....
How did you get that job?
Actually they found me on harri.com
All I did was go to the interview and be myself. And apparently I was what they were looking for.

What is it like working in that environment?
Working for a cruise line is very different than working in a regular bar.
It does get rocky and you do break glasses more often but it's so much fun.

You also have to be very formal and on point with their rules and regulations, which are very strict by the way (they have requirements from the way your hair looks to the type of rubber on your shoes and length of your shirt sleeves).

Can't say more. Yes, you do sign a confidentiality agreement.

How/When To Ask For A Raise?

Steven Gallanter - I am a bartender at Ramrod-machine in Boston, MA who poured his first drink in 1982. I have also managed and worked in other positions in those 30 years. Cheers, http://stevegallanter.wordpress.com

Steven Says:
"When to ask" is best done after you have done a bunch of fill-ins, especially if they are not your usual situation.

"What to ask" is most effective when you ask to work more often. In this way you can be perceived as wishing to add your value more often.

"How often to ask" is the toughest.
It is very easy to irritate schedule makers with this request, yet you have to put yourself into the mix. Asking every other week is the safest bet.

Joel Scholtens Lindsay – http://www. earthbar.org
I have spent approximately 22 years in the industry.
I hail from Sydney Australia and have worked in Australia, Europe, Asia and America.

Working as a bar back, glassy, bartender, Mixologist, flair bartender, event bartender, head bartender, manager, represented liquor brands and corporate brands, consultant.

I own my own consultancy business www.earthbar.org and am currently Mixologist/ bar consultant to the Taj Palace Hotel, Hotel New Delhi and have many other bar professionals working in for me in the Industry in Asia.

How Do You Talk To Your Boss?
Talking to your boss can be intimidating.
Tell us your stories, successful or not, and what you learned.

The truth is most people see life from their own perspective and over value themselves, I have also been guilty during my career of thinking I was so much better than I was and (I am awesome) ha ha.

Now I'm a business owner and money doesn't grow on trees, most bartenders think the boss earns so much money when the reality is the boss has so much debt.

Your boss owns a business and is probably going to hire a manager not based on quality but who he can relate and communicate well with.

The minute you think you deserve a promotion your work suffers, normally you start creating disharmony in the team and you are no longer the asset you think you are.

The truth is most bars have a high turnover rate and if you're patient opportunities will come.

After the 9/11 terrorist attacks I was working as a Bartender with the Hilton Heathrow.
Thirty percent of the staff got fired in one week. I was the only F & B employee that had one job in the bar. I was basically running the department, with the title of bartender.

I never complained, I never moaned. I just preformed and I then got poached to the Hilton Trafalgar as Assistant Manager and, five months later, that bar won best bar in London.

Work hard, be patient, don't turn into a negative influence on your team and doors will open.

When Do You Ask For A Raise?

When you're willing to start working to get it and want your boss to know you're interested.

What to ask?

What do I need to improve to get promoted?
Let's you know what your boss wants and lets your boss know you're interested. How often to ask?

Once upfront, then ask questions like I did this how would you have done it?
Show the boss you respect him/her and want to learn from them.

In my world I am the most important person, It simple human nature, I like to feel respected and important, I like being around people who make me feel good about myself.

I also like people who work hard for me, do as I ask and give 100%.

Did you have a plan? What was it?
The best plan I ever saw was a friend Gerard (my bar manager at the time) who went to the GM with a four-page point-by-point document saying when I have achieved every objective on this list, I want my next promotion.

Did you have a letter with you describing what you wanted and why you deserve it?
If you need to give your boss a letter to sell yourself, you haven't built up a good enough relationship with the boss to deserve a promotion.

Promotion means being a leader and leaders have confidence.

If you're a manager, what advice can you give to employees?
Always seek to improve yourself and get better.

The success in my career has not come by asking for promotions it come from bettering my skills and learning.

Tore Berger Bartender, Waiter, Manager, Consultant.
Over 25 years in the industry.
Bar and beverage menu planning/settings. Counselor/teacher/judge for waiter diploma students, since 2008. Judge in drink/bar technique competitions.

Lectures/training in bar, wine, spirits, service. Writer of beverage articles in various settings
(Papers, magazines, company letters, bartender web sites + +)

Tore Says:
* Hard work, showing skills, and guest feedback. That gives a win-win situation.

The business: The right person at the best/right time, and a happier, more satisfied employee.

The business are the employees, the employees are the business.

Your First Shift. Suggestions on how to do great?
Be humble but secure. Let your work and guests "talk" for you!

Cruise ships are normally part of BIG Companies, and have 100 % manuals on everything.

Everybody has to make the cocktails exactly the same way. Hygiene is No 1, and you are always a part of a team.

If you want to do something extra,
i.e. a new creation, the code is: Inform both guests and colleagues what you do.

On a ship it is mostly team efforts that decide, then use your new creation cocktails in internal or company competitions.

Also remember that flair is for the special occasions, and that the uniform is the company's ID.

Work hard, get good guest feedback, and you can get your own cabin and head barman job...

How Do You Move From Bartender Into Management? What advice do you have? Show what you can, work hard, always work extra when asked, go to competitions, show both yourself and the company, make menu suggestions...
Eventually things start to turn, and then people/bosses start asking YOU.

What are the "Cons" of being a manager?
What are some difficulties moving from bartender to management?
You are suddenly your colleagues' boss.
Be aware of that, and think of the team as a whole! Use coaching when needed.

Do you have any good stories to share?
People forget easily. It can be funny to be boss of people you used to work with.

As a manager I don't get tipped, of course, and when you ask if the tip is good, these days it's always the same: "No, it's bad. Things are not like it used to be..."

Then you start thinking of the manager you had before you got his job.

What answer did you give him when he asked about the tip?
Yes, it goes on and on!

Andy Lakatos - After 8 years in the mobile bartenders business, Andy has founded an on-line store where you can buy those swanky, glowing tables & bars you see in Hollywood nightclubs & celebrity weddings. http://barchefs.com/

Andy Says:
Re: Asking for raises.
I usually just fire people when this starts popping up. Just kidding haha. Ask when you know your boss would rather keep you than lose you.

Make yourself more valuable to the company.
Take on tasks that decrease the owner's workload.

Don't take breaks in front of owner but away.
Do not constantly ask how to do things and learn yourself.
Lastly, buy owner presents and chocolate (optional)

Mary Dunn - For five years, I've worked in an ocean-front, open-air bar. The average age customer is 40-75, seriously!

Mary Says:
I think if you pull your weight, show your worth, you shouldn't have to ask for any of these.

Scott Says:
In a perfect world with a great manager who's totally on the ball, I agree with you Mary.

Unfortunately, even with those perfect conditions, managers are usually overworked so...within reason of course, "The Squeaky Wheel gets the grease".

If people don't learn to promote themselves, respectfully but with confidence, others with possibly less qualifications than you will reap the rewards.

Robert Kiyosaki is a world-renowned best-selling author and speaker, etc.

He said to be a Best Selling Author, you not only have to create high quality products, you have to be a "Best SELLER".

If you don't have both sides of the coin, then you won't be as successful as you could be. Mr. Kiyosaki was talking about selling books but I think the lesson applies to employees in all industries.

My experiences have proved to me
that even if we feel that we
shouldn't "have to" ask for what we want,
if we do not find a way to do it,
respectfully but with confidence,
we often will not get what we want.

But someone else will.

So, the question stands:
What can we do to increase the odds?
What has worked for you/Not worked for you? etc.

Gioia Bartalo -Manager/Bartender for three years at Beef 'O' Brady's

Gioia Says:
"Respectfully but with confidence" is the best thing I've heard in a while, Scott!

So many times people fall into a situation of entitlement, which just irritates management even more.
By proving you are a valuable asset to the company, they will work to keep you on staff rather than watch you find new employment.

I've found that when people ask for additional shifts, it's helpful to keep a log of tasks they had done that weren't part of the "job description".

This way when management asks why you deserve it, you have direct proof.

It's also important not to get tangled up in thinking you are doing everything because you take on a few more organizational and cleaning tasks – it is your job, after all.

**"Selling" yourself
is also an important concept.**

**Your brand
is what people know you for,
and how to get places.**

It's important to know both how to develop it and how to showcase it.

Rhonda Bloom – Owner for two years
Hi Scott, I'd love to be involved in your project. Good Luck 😃
Rhonda www.facebook.com/MudslingersBOB

Rhonda Says:
Re: Asking for a raise
As an employer, when employees see sales increase or think they have been there long enough, they are compelled to ask for a raise.

Why not? I don`t blame them. It actually shows me that they are noticing.

However, as a business owner, it is not always best or possible to agree to a raise.
So I use it as an opportunity to set an active goal for them and the company.
This will help drive them more.

It has also been my experience that instead of agreeing to a raise, I like to set milestones. When we can hit a milestone, I offer bonuses.

Employees understand that small business has a degree of challenges that don`t always allow for us to give big pay raises but when we can meet certain levels and milestones I can and do give a pat on the back and show my appreciation with monetary bonuses.

As an employer, I actually had staff approach me who prepared their own proposals and/or a title position that they desired and why they deserved it and what they could further bring to the company.

I love that. It shows their tenacity and drive.

I loved the initiative that it took to approach me.
This allowed my staff to invest of themselves to our company and show they cared about the company and their jobs.

It allowed something to be brought to the table and discussed and evaluated and construct the needs of what the employees saw as a need for the company.

I appreciated this aspect. With a little tweaking and evaluating the proposals everyone was a winner. It actually made the staff more accountable for their work and drive sales and meet goals. WIN WIN.

Don't ask unless you truly feel you deserve it. Be prepared to provide reasons other than "I have been here a long time."

Provide examples of how you have helped increase sales and your success stories.
How you are an asset and how you can be a bigger asset.
What additional roles you are willing to take on.
Ideas for saving $$$.

"Larry" Gilario Guevara
My name 's Larry Guevara, a.k.a. "The Saint" because of my seminary backgrounds back in the days. I used to work for TGIFriday's Manila, Philippines as a flair bartender and in-store coach from 2003 to 2005 but I'm now working as a **Cruise Lines Flair Bartender for Celebrity Cruises.**

And when people ask me why I chose to be a bartender instead of becoming a priest - well, I realized there are more spirits behind the bar than in the church.

I've worked for another cruise lines (Louis Cruise Lines) prior for four years wherein our itinerary mostly included the Mediterranean. I started working in the cruise lines industry from 2005 up to the present.

I represented my store at the inter-store TGIFriday's Bartending Championship for two years and came out first runner-up during my first ever competition in 2003 plus I also won the Original Cocktail Concoction.

During my second competition I got the "Best in Pour Test" award and emerged as "the crowd favourite."

It was through these that I received numerous invitations to give up talks, seminars and flair bartending demos in the different parts of the Philippine islands, and appeared in national broadsheets, magazines and even appeared on a series of national TV programs.

While taking up Bar & Beverage Management I class, I saw some of classmates flipping bottles and that ignited my passion for flair bartending. The rest, they say, is history.

Larry Says:
My "guiding philosophy" in life
(regardless whether I'm working behind the bar or not)
comes from the Chinese proverb that said:

**"Make happy
those who are near
and
those who are far
will come."**

Did you make it as a bartender right away?
Just to give you a short background of my bartending career,
I started applying for the bartender position at TGIFriday's
since the beginning of 2000 but I didn't get the job until 2003.

The thing was, even though I had the guts and the basic
knowledge of becoming a bartender I later realized that
I lacked a lot on experience and bartending skills which
explains why I didn't make the cut.

But that didn't stop me from pursuing though my dream
of becoming a bartender.
In fact, like the story of Michael Jordan when he didn't
make the cut in his sophomore years to play basketball,
the experience taught me a lot of lessons and made me
even more passionate and determined to pursue my
bartending career.
Through research, constant practice and a lot of heart
poured into my new found calling, everything finally paid
off when I finally got a flair bartender job at TGIFriday's
Malate in 2003.

There is really no secret in getting the better shift, the promotion or even the raise.
It all depends on how much you prove yourself.

I honestly admit that "flair" has been one of my strongest points since I really spend a lot of time perfecting and practicing it for years.

But apart from that, I also love to read, do research and learn more about our products.

Knowledge is just within our reach and with the advent of the internet and the continuous development of technology.

**There is no reason for us to be stagnant
or stale
when it comes to knowledge.**

It's how we make use of it
that separates
any great bartender
from
the ordinary guy.

Some consider bartending
simply as a "gig",
while people
like us who are passionate and dedicated to the craft,
consider bartending
as a
PROFESSION.

The question is: "Which side of the fence are you in?"

The CHOICE is definitely YOURS.
Jancy Nightingale – Eight Years in the Industry, Bartender, Designer, Student. I've been in the food and beverage industry eight years acting as a hostess, busser, server, barista, and bartender. I pursued a bartending certificate in 2010 and it's been one of the best investments I've made for myself.

Jancy Says:
Two words: Work hard.

- Offer to take any shift, and take them even if you don't want or need them.

- Be the person they call first because they know you will say yes and you are reliable.

  If you say you want them and you'll take any shift, but then turn down shifts when they offer them, you are saying you don't really want them.

- Offer to come in on your own time for miscellaneous reasons.

Make sure you have done
everything in your power to prepare yourself
for any window of opportunity,
so if it opens
you are ready and more than capable
of jumping through
(and staying through!).

- Never be a headache. Nobody wants a headache, ever.

- Face time with the owner or manager or whoever makes the call or has influence is always good.

- Learn how the system works and how you can play it.

- Don't limit yourself to just one place.

- Always be honest with your bosses.

- Ask if it's okay if you take an additional bar job.
  Assure them it won't interfere or compete with their interests.

- It's always easier to find work while you have a job.
  Network while you have work, make friends and talk to people.
  Get to know them and let them know you.

- Keep your reputation sacred where ever you are.
  Even big cities have small bar scenes.

  Everybody knows everybody or knows someone who does.

- Ask what you need to do to advance?

Keep in mind nothing has happened until it has, just because you are promised something doesn't mean it's going to happen.

Keep working with a stellar record before and after.

Let people know you are serious.

Stacie Little – My name is Stacie Little and I'm from Jamaica. I entered the bartending arena at the age of 17, practically sneaking into it as my mom wasn't so approving of it. Bartending is a undiscovered art here in Jamaica. The mentality is anyone can be a bartender and a bartender is just a little man or woman scantily dressed behind a corner bar in the community who just pours a shot of over-proof rum.

What are The Best Ways to Ask For/Get a Raise, Promotion & Better Shifts?
Firstly you have to prove yourself to your manager that you are capable of managing the bar and controlling guests' flow for the night.

Once you prove that then it will be easier to get anything that you want.

But expect nothing if you are a slacker.

Renae Tsukamoto – 7 years in the industry. I'm still one of the young'uns in the industry, but I've managed to figure it out pretty quickly, however not without some static on my way up. I moved up from host to server, server to bartender, and bartender to manager. Once I fell into the world of flair, I became addicted, hence why I made the move to Las Vegas.

Getting to work with some of the best in the industry is truly incredible and still blows my mind that its actually happening. I'm glad to have broken some stereotypes (as far as being so young, female, being a mixologist and flair bartender, etc.) and can't wait to keep breaking more. ☺

Renae Says:
RE: Raises
In all honesty, usually people don't ask for promotions or raises in this industry. They happen based on performance, and even when bars and restaurants do "auditions" to move up, they already have an idea of who they want to promote or put in the position, they just "have to give everyone a fair chance."

I see it more as you want management to ask YOU if you would be interested in moving up, rather than you asking THEM to do so. The only way to do that is to perform well.

Mike 'Bullfrog' Summers – Hospitality Industry Specialist – 22-year vet of the Bar Biz, 27-year vet of the service industry. Part Flairtender, Part Beertender, Part Mixologist, High-volume, to low-volume, 5-star to no-star. Shameless self-promoter, skilled Innovator, and soon to be Entrepreneur. Worked from bottom to the top, held every position in between. Union and non-union positions, employee and management posts. Nightclub to dive bar.

1) I have always set myself apart with a mix of skill, good work ethic, personality, and solid leadership traits to the point that most times a start a new job I am approached by management for a shift lead/supervisory/management position with corresponding wage increase within three months of start date

2) As a manager the best advice I can give to employees is to always work hard, try your best, come to work prepared, and to NEVER be afraid or too proud to ask for help/accept help when you are in 'the weeds'.

Philip Gillivan – 28 years in the industry.
Hi Scott, I would love to get involved with some of my experiences from this side of the pond. Philip is a Pub Consultant specialist who works with Pubs who want to Increase Turnover, Reduce Overheads and Increase Net Profit.

Philip also works with individuals who wish to own their own or lease their own pubs, helping them to avoid expensive learning curves. Philip's experience over the last twenty eight years in the pub trade has given him the expertise to help other pub owners and managers bring their businesses to a new level of efficiency and profitability.

Philip Says:
In my opinion the best way to get a raise is to demonstrate to your boss how you are going to bring added value to the business.

The days are gone when you get a raise just because you are there so long.

Have a look and see some of the tasks your boss does personally and see if they will delegate that to you. If you can lighten their workloads then you are adding value to your own position. The raise will come or if you decide to move on you have a new skill.

Scott Says:

That's a good point Philip. Being assertive/creative problem-solver that makes your boss's life/job easier is definitely a way to prove that you are a more valuable employee than the avg. person who just clocks in and clocks out without looking around to see how to make things better.

J.J. Jackie Elsbury – Over 12 years in the industry. (Now In Las Vegas)

J.J. is a well-known flair bar tender and bar manager in the service industry in Utah.

He has managed restaurants front of the house and back of the house.
Has brought the standard of bartending to a higher level using flair mixology and showmanship.

J.J. is fluent in English and Spanish. He oversees bar operation and insures maximum profit, manage inventory, scheduling, regulatory compliance with the D.A.B.C. and health department. J.J. has completed his schooling with a degree in business management.

Overall, J.J. prides himself on customer service and making sure there is a fun and profitable work environment for everyone.

J.J. Says:
What to do when asking for raise or promotion.
This is a very hard question to answer.

Because working in this industry you have a lot of dishonesty, partying, alcoholism, etc., etc., if you are going to ask for a promotion you want to make sure you are a very honest person who has priorities and is looking for advancement.

Make sure you know what u are talking about before jumping into the fire.

The things a manager looks for are theft, portioning, and loss if you have all those under control with suggestive selling and building your clientele then go for it.

If you have a bad attitude about your job and you are not a team player?
Then you probably shouldn't.

Remember you have to be confident and secure with yourself before anything.
"That does not mean cocky!" LOL.

So You Want To Work On A Cruise Ship?

FYI - Many if not most cruise ship bartenders are from Non- North American countries.

Gilario "Larry" Guevara – Manila, Philippines as a flair bartender and in-store coach from 2003 to 2005 but I'm now working as a **Cruise Lines Flair Bartender for Celebrity Cruises.**

And when people ask me why I chose to be a bartender instead of becoming a priest - well, I realized there are more spirits behind the bar than in the church.

When I moved to Celebrity Cruises in 2009, I was already seven years bartending and had four years shipboard experience. However, by God's grace or by fate I got hired on Celebrity Cruises as a Bar storekeeper and not as bartender.

I was told by my agent that I should take the job and eventually apply for the bartending position once I get on-board the ship.

Being a first-timer on Celebrity and with no one to guide me, I took the offer hoping that I would indeed work behind the bar once I get on-board the cruise ship.

Little did I know that I would actually be working for the Inventory Management Department and not the Bar Department.

To cut the long story short, I have to spend my six-month contract working in coveralls with nothing else do except receive pallets of bar items during loading day; arrange them inside the bar storeroom; issue requisitions, and; take care of inventory.

Up to this day, I still consider that experience as the most "devastating" if not "heart-breaking" part in my career.

Not because I didn't get the position right away but because I was told it was just my first contract and I couldn't shift right away to the bar department.

Apparently though, when I passed the examinations and went through all the necessary interviews for the bartending position and yet I ended up doing another "job" which I was actually over-qualified for.

But being an optimistic person that I've always been, I still treasure that situation as one of my "most humbling experience" and feel so thankful that I went through it because from that I experience I learned more about more bar items like wines, more spirits and liqueurs and, for the most part, I learned how to drive a forklift in no time.

Now, I work at one of the busiest bars on the ship (the Martini Bar) where we don't only make good tips but we also get to have fun with our guests.

Personally, I'm so thankful because all my years of practicing, researching and learning the true value of flair behind the bar have paid off.

Flair in the ship is now becoming a rule rather than an exception.
My point is, more and more flair bartenders are getting jobs because of their extra skills as compared to a bartender who can't flair.

In my present company, for example, they realized the importance of competing with the shore-side establishments like in Las Vegas so the company finally decided to bring the concept of flair bartending in ships thus they added the concept of the Martini Bar which is actually a flair bar.

Apparently, bartending in ships is way more different in a land-based bar or restaurant although the same basic knowledge and skills have to be acquired first in order to succeed as a bartender.

Like in a chain restaurant, the bartenders creativity in preparing cocktails can sometimes be limited because of the company rules and standards.

However, this shouldn't stop anyone from pushing the envelope because like any other profession bartending is a continued process of learning, of trial and error.

Working in cruise ships as compared to any land-based establishment is not an easy job.

It is more demanding; involves longer hours and a lot of 'special cleaning' most especially in the US ports where the United States Public health inspectors get onboard the ship to check whether the standards on sanitation and safety of the ship are followed and met.

It is a grueling job being in the cruise ship too because of the trainings and the drills that all crew members have to undergo throughout the contract.

What is your signature move if any?
- The "foot swipe" like a breakdance flair move. The "London Bridge" with a bottle and tin exchange from between my legs and a whole lot more.…..
Hehehehehe…Check out my videos in YouTube! Search for speakeasy101.

- Life is a very unpredictable reality so for the moment I just want to go with the flow and let the tides of life lead me.

Working in the cruise lines has been one of the best part of my career so I guess I'll keep on travelling for now to see the world and enjoy life to the fullest. Cheers!

Interview With A Consulate – Richie Cruise

14 years in industry. Hotel and Restaurant Administration at the University of the Philippines-Diliman.

He realized that BARTENDING was the career path to take after seeing Tom Cruise's classic movie, "Cocktails", and has never looked back.

Scott Says: Richie is quite the inspiration to many in the bartending and flair bartending world. I invite you to check out his FB page https://www.facebook.com/richie.cruise?fref=ts and see what he's up to now. He has graciously allowed me to share his article with you here. Thanks Richie and good luck with all you do ☺

Richie Says:
So why come up with a blog like this one?

Well, it's really pretty simple. I would just like to tell everybody out there that it's not a big deal…period.

Let me elaborate…For overseas contract workers reading this blog, we all know that if we will have a job outside the country, the most dreaded part of our requirements will come when we are going to apply for VISA…for definition purposes, this visa will let us pass through a certain country. Let's take the United States for example.

I was able to ask some seniors of mine in the industry about it and they say there is a very big difference of getting a visa before and now especially when the 911 thing happened.

O, but before we continue let me back track a bit …you need to apply for a passport first before getting a visa.

This one you have to accomplish by going to the Department of Foreign Affairs somewhere in Libertad, Pasay. If you come early, it will only take you around a day to finish everything and come back for your passport after two days I think.

Do not bother going to fixers. There's really not much of a difference in fee and speed of processing…in fact going thru the normal process and being an obedient citizen is more affordable.

After getting a passport, of course you need a recruitment or a manning agency which will help you in processing your WORKING Visa.
But then again, if you do not wish to work in another country but rather just tour, then just go the US Embassy website for further information for that's another story.

If you are an OFW, your agency will process everything for you. All you have to do is pay the processing fee and procure an application form from the bank.

Now we are in the meaty stuff … this piece of paper before used to cost $100.

But now … one must pay in peso and mind you it goes up steadily … even if the peso is stronger … the price of this paper would be far different from the conversion table.

Having said this information, this pretty much would make a good motivation to pass your interview so that you won't waste your money "big time."

After all the paper works have been accomplished and submitted, your agency will give a "briefing" on how your interview will be like.

Ok, so your agency tells you that you have to memorize this and that but expect the unexpected …

And so on the day of your interview you have to be there an hour before (bring all your documents and don't bring ANY electronic devices for you will not be allowed to bring it in the embassy premises.

Now, in case you do bring it there are some peddlers outside that can take care of your precious item while you are inside for a fee) since you still have to pass your documents, do finger print scanning and wait for your number is called.

The waiting game is the hardest of all because you came prepared only to be listening to stories of other people.

In getting a visa there are two types of applicants: the first timers and the renewals. Some say if you are going to be renewed it would be much easier…do not count your chickens just yet …

Now once it's your turn, your interview will only be two minutes at the most!!! Wow!!! Then right there and then you will know if you PASSED or you got DENIED.

A passing mark means you get a green slip while if you are denied you will get a blue slip.

Now, how do you pass your interview?
Actually, there is no sure formula …
but here are three tips that would help:

1. **Learn to speak and understand ENGLISH**.

    You will be interviewed by a foreigner so you have to dance with the music …
    you have no choice … you want to enter their country so learn what the Romans do … but in this case just focus on the language … culture is another topic.
    In doing this you can express yourself freely and with confidence which shows in your gestures and your eyes, and the better your grasp of the language the better you can play with the words.

    Sometimes since some are not really that well versed this is the part where they fail.

2. Know your job well.

If you do this all questions that will be thrown will be a piece of cake.

Basically you will be asked about your job. If you know your job well you can pick any aspect of it and explain it to your consul who might not have an idea of what is it all about.

But this goes hand in hand with tip number 1 which I already explained.

I remember one consul asked me, how do you open a bottle of wine? I said,
"Oh, that's easy!!" (Yadada yadada … and I passed. :)

3. Be confident and sincere.

Confidence is different from being a smart aleck we can define confidence here as being sure of your answers because you've gone through step 1 and 2 and this would help you to look at the interviewer directly since eye to eye is very important.

It also projects that you are sincere in applying for a job and you do not have a hidden agenda.

And do not forget your proper etiquette and that honest to goodness SMILE :)

As a final word, you can expect the unexpected…but if you put the three tips in your system, there is nothing to worry about.

Yet, anything can happen…despite doing the three tips you still flunk …
learn to accept your FATE … you can always try again or maybe working outside isn't for you … remember … "Acceptance is the key to moving forward."

Cheers!!!

For more info about What it's like to work on a cruise ship,
check out these articles…

http://www.cruiselinesjobs.
com/a-day-in-the-life-of-a-bartender/

http://www.travelandleisure.com/
articles/i-was-a-cruise-ship-bartender

http://www.foxnews.com/travel/2012/01/09/
working-on-cruise-ship/

How To Get A Job As A Brand Ambassador

Kyle Dill - Brand Ambassador

Kyle Says:
It's all kind of relative – don't you think? Given that liquor or spirits companies are large, small, some have budget to hire, some outsource to other companies for representation.

In Colorado, it's not that difficult to become a 'brand ambassador' given that you have the right tools, networks, and know-how as the distilleries are a rather dense population here locally.

One of the biggest mistakes that brand ambassadors make on the small batch privately owned level is that you are not a face that gets to travel and live the typical 'dream of the ambassadorship' – rather, your position is sales and you're also required to distribute the product after you sell it.

There are National, International yes – but also local and even smaller –
Independent positions available to look at.

I would inspire those interested to first look at your most local spirits producers on the independent level, great introduction into the field, often with greater responsibility and opportunity for upward growth within the company, or beyond.

I could go through differences all day between large and small companies, but it's always good to step back and realize what job you're signing up for when you do.

It's the biggest local mistake for the bartender transitioning to ambassador, is not being aware of your duties before you take the position.

For reference, I'm the chief editor of Industry America Media
www.Industry-Denver.com and write about food, drinks, and industry culture.

In addition to that I've also represented two Colorado spirits producers in the field and once in marketing as well.

Those brands are now handled by my team at Ethanol Strategies and would love to give anybody as much advice as I can. www.ethanolStrategies.com

Oh, and the how-to?
Go get em, seek em out, tweet em, e-mail em,
go everywhere you think they might be and become familiar.
Make the effort.

Héctor F Hernández Fernández
VP Sales & Marketing at AMBHAR Global Spirits, LLC

Hector Says:
Hi Scott. The most important thing to me is to be 100% convinced of what the brand stands for, what it delivers to consumers and trade as well as fully understand their elements that make it somewhat unique.

This same applies for the company that supports such brand.

Once you have that, the rest depends on your personal and professional skills to "become the face of the brand".

Experienced Brand Ambassador – Wants to remain nameless

One thing to keep in mind about the whiskey ambassador positions, as well as some of the vodka and liqueur roles, is that the trends seems to be reverting back to have someone from the spirit's country of origin represent it.

You will see that all of the Irish whiskeys
(Tullamore Dew, Kilbeggan, Jameson)
now have very young people from Ireland representing the brands.

Even Bushmills, which to this point has been represented by the various Diageo Master of Whisky has taken one of the MOW who is from Ireland and made him the National Ambassador for the brand.

I have seen the same happen for Scotch as well.
So keep in mind that you may not get the job because you do not have an accent.

A company won't publicly admit this, but I have had executives with suppliers tell me as such.

Also age is plying a bigger and bigger part in their hiring decisions.

Guys like me, though having more experience, come with a higher price tag and are seen as not being part of the young, hip mixology culture.

You can hire a young person with little experience, train them on brand knowledge and give them an expense account to spend in bars, and it works out a lot cheaper. Oh well.

Ulric Nijs
Brat-tender for about 16 years, started in Japan and travelled across the world in bars and distilleries.

I eventually became a trainer and brand ambassador for some of the big boys for the past five years in the Middle East and Southeast Asia.

Ulric Says:
I LOVE the industry, and a strong believer in the "less-is-more" philosophy!

The more complicated your drink the less likely you are to link/relate to your consumers. Drinking and making drinks is about fun and relaxing above all… I am very much against the term "Mixology" or "star-tenders" as it goes against the core values of the job;

Above all we are here for the guests NOT for our own ego and for the drinks (these come as an added benefit).

The bowtie does not define the bartender!

 **Dominik M.J. Schachtsiek** www. opinionated-alchemist.com Bar & beverage veteran & blogger.

Worked/Works as Bar Manager & Beverage Manager in renowned 5-star deluxe properties – Repositioning bars, developing food & beverage concepts, training staff, developing cocktail program, promotions, menu design, day to day operations with guests in focus.

His knowledge spans from classic to contemporary mixology, his expertise lies in spirits, cigars, cocktails

and bar management and he also has a big focus on developing the culinary side of the bar. Now in Dubai and Abu Dhabi.
www.linkedin.com/profile/
view?id=31439816&locale=en_US&trk=tyah

Dominik Says:
I think the conditions are widely changing, depending on how big a brand is.

To work for Diageo reserve brands, Bacardi or Jack Daniels will be better paid (and usually it will be a full time job) than to work for a boutique brand.

Also it differs if you are a regional, a national or a global brand ambassador.

 **Peter Benjamin**
I am a brand consultant and financial advisor with over 20 years' experience building brands and managing high net worth clients.

My Brand Success have been Sparkling NUVO (sold to Diageo)- www.sparklingnuvo.com and Hpnotiq (sold to Heaven Hill) www.hpnotiq.com with acquisitions to the tune of over 150 Million and represent pop culture icons.

2012 Nuvo was the third largest imported brand. I created and managed a stellar team and we believe in proper tools and training to get the best results.

We made drinking fruity drinks cool for mainstream and opened a new generation to the market.

Peter Says:
My philosophy is simple: I believe in the management before the product.
A great product can sell itself to a point but it takes a great team to succeed.
There is no I in Team.

I am building a lifestyle platform called MyOffices® which brings location based living to life.

As a national manager for a successful brand the best advice I can give is to have a working relationship with establishments and bartenders at all the major venues.

Brand ambassadors have to be able to navigate the trendy locations to showcase the brands they wish to represent.

A quality team of young people with great personalities is always great to have as well. It's always a team effort to promote successfully. Best regards.

D'Nai Walker
10 Years in this industry: hospitality in general 10, Spirits – 4
Current job title: Key Account Manager. Worked as a bartender, promotional model, market manager for promo agency.

Key Account Manager at Remy Cointreau.

D'Nai Says:

**There are always options in life.
If you don't like something,
change it!**

I've been around many brand ambassadors within the company I work for and others.

In my experience, most brand ambassadors are high tier bartenders/mixologists, that have advanced knowledge about the history of spirits & cocktails.

They know a lot about the process of how different spirits are made and have dedicated their time to learning more about cocktail culture.

What are the "Pros" of the job?
Travel within your designated region and usually to the distillery you represent, being the "face" of the brand, meeting other like-minded people in the spirits world, having a budget to do special events, etc.

What are the "Cons" of the job?
Travel. Also, getting used to dealing with a corporate structure.

Depending on the company, there can be more paperwork than most bartenders are used to: tracking and recapping activities, conference calls, managing budgets, expense reports, and sticking to the deadlines that corporate demands.

What exactly are the duties of a brand ambassador?
Usually training bartenders and trying to get them behind your brands, relaying the story behind your brand, representing your brand at trade & consumer events and help get your products on menus.

What kind and level of experience is required?
Advanced knowledge of spirits, public speaking, self-starter.

Local rep?
Typically you aren't expected to know quite as much, because there is most likely a regional or national ambassador above you.

National Rep?
Lots of travel, larger events....Tales of the Cocktail, etc

International Rep?
I only know one, he travels quite a bit for international spirits competitions, but is usually based at his home distillery.

What if You have a lot bar professional bartending experience, but no professional sales gigs?
That's not a problem, bartenders are salesmen!
The company will give you some (usually minimal) training.

How would one highlight a resume to present for a brand ambassador job? Highlight you knowledge of spirits and cocktails.

These guys usually know a lot about the history of how the classics came to be,

What kind of monetary compensation range is there?
Varies from company to company, local BAs are often part-time and hired through an agency vs. the actual company.

How do you get paid?
Usually a set salary....sometimes per event executed.

Starting salary/wage?
Depends...part-time 30k, full-time 65k-80k.
This can depend on amount of travel required, etc.

Hours expected?
Hours can be demanding, especially Oct-Dec. Weekends and nights are a must.

How do you choose a company?
Choose something you truly enjoy and
can speak passionately about.....
you'll be drinking nothing but that for a while!

How do you approach them?
Most companies will post on sites like <u>www.bevforce.com</u>, you can try making a presentation, but getting a meeting in front of the right people will probably be difficult.
If they want an ambassador, they will budget for one in advance.

Anything to watch out for?
Most people only stay ambassadors for 2-3 years, unless you are a global ambassador.
I think there is a bit of a burn out factor.

Dean Callan: Be Yourself, Everyone Else is Taken

Since getting my job as a global brand ambassador, I am finding more and more people asking **'how did you get that job?'**
My answer to this is simple, I don't really know.

Out of shot, those silver sleeves are rolled up, Miami Vice style.

What I do know, is that I have always followed a few key 'mantras'.

I wouldn't say that I really have rules but more so inspirations.

I have tried to list a few quotes that have inspired me and my interpretation of them. Hopefully they'll be useful for you too!

1. **"Be Yourself, everyone else is taken"** – Oscar Wilde.

Being yourself means more than just having your own opinion and voicing it, it means being true to who you are in every aspect of your life.

If you don't like being stuffy and wearing a suit all the time don't work in a super fancy hotel, if you don't like customers then become a chef, don't take it out on the guests.

The idea that someone is naturally talented in the service industry is a myth, they are simply comfortable in their shoes, working in the right job and have the requisite skills to pay the bills.

You need all three to be good at your job and happy in it, only then will you even be considered for ambassadorship.

2. **"I was out of touch, but it wasn't because I didn't know enough.**
    I just knew too much" - Gnarls Barkley.

One of the best things you can do in this industry is know stuff.
It builds confidence, helps round your skills and makes for good shop talk with colleagues.

One of the worst things you can do is only apply this healthy appetite for learning to random bullshit facts, start learning about your guests, why do they come in?

What are they passionate about?
Do they like Pińa Coladas and getting caught in the rain?

Not everyone wants to listen to you talk about esters, congeners, the history of the Pineapple or the increasing use of anaerobic reactors by spirit production facilities.

I have a one track mind (albeit easily distracted) and it's hard to think of anything outside my own interests, but to really make conversation I need to take a vested interest in what other people might want to talk about.

I am still learning to pace myself, stop getting too in depth and chewing peoples ears off.

Don't bother with conversations about politics, religion or "original cocktail trends" unless you are speaking to Jacob Briars.
Then you might learn something from a true genius of interesting conversation and knowing his audience.

3. **"The creative adult is the child who never grew up"**
   Not sure where I got this from, but it works for me (and Peter Pan).

This is a tricky one really because not everyone is creative, some people say I am creative but as a matter of fact I am not. I just like a challenge, and I like to have fun.

I like to think of something that I can't already do, and see if I can learn to do it.

It's like the old saying "necessity is the mother of all creation", if you decide to do something you think is extremely difficult, and truly work at it, you will be forced to think creatively.

You just need a driving force to kick you in the butt sometimes, competitions are a perfect example of a driving force.

Some of the best flavour combinations, techniques, presentations and characters I have ever seen where in competitions. People are pushing themselves because they want to win, this is great and I whole heartedly embrace the competition scene, although in my mind there is something better, a more powerful driving force.

It's the inner child, it's the part of you that starts a sentence with
"what if… ?"
or
"imagine if we…"

Being confident enough to throw an idea out into the world without fear of rejection or embarrassment is the real key to pushing yourself, because it's you doing the pushing, you are the one getting excited about your next big challenge.

4. **"You're good, kid, but as long as I'm around, you're only second best"**
   - Lancey Howard (Character from the Cincinnati Kid)

No matter how good you are, how hard you work, how much you study, how many competitions you win…

No matter what job you land, how much money you make, how far you travel, how many people you know or places you have seen…

There is always someone better.

They may be at a different stage in their career, or maybe they live in some far away corner of the earth that you will never visit.

They are still better. Get over it.

If you start thinking you are the best, or that you know everything, you are heading backwards.

If you can't shake that feeling send me an e-mail or call me, I am happy to administer a slap in the face. If I am otherwise engaged (or on the other side of the planet) then do what I do. Look for the people who inspire you, the ones you look up to and keep in touch with them. They should bring you back to earth, I have a long list of them (my girlfriend is at the top, she rocks my world).

If you are having trouble finding someone to look up to I can suggest a few, John Gakuru, Jacob Briars, Gary

Regan, Jason Crawley, Marco Faraone, Sven and Amber Almenning, Barry Chalmers, Raj Nagra, Justin McKenzie, Jim Wrigley, Stuart Hudson, Mathew Hewitt, Hugh Paten-Smith, Gregor De Guyther, Zdenek Kastanek, Lee Linford, Dale De Groff, Jim Meehan, Dushan Zarich, Jake Burger, Tony C, Nick Van Tiel, just to mention a few.

My list of inspirations is too long for the page, and my reasons might be unique to each individual but I am still humbled and inspired by them every day.

5. **No amount of experimentation can prove me right, a simple experiment can prove me wrong.** – Albert Einstein.

The last and most important piece of advice is to take into account what I have said and consider me wrong. Then work toward proving me wrong, depending on your point of view you might just succeed, seemingly rendering this entire reading experience useless.

But in the process of proving that I know nothing, take note of what you learn for yourself, and about yourself.

That is the only real way to learn, by doing your own work, and coming to your own conclusions.

Everyone is unique and we all learn differently, try to remember that, it's useful for when you are teaching someone new, give them the patience they deserve. Oh and to get you started on proving how full of shit I am, I made this all up, none of it can be backed up in any classic cocktail books. Except for perhaps <u>Joy of Mixology,Gary Regan knows everything, buy his book</u>

How do you choose a company?
Always make sure you are representing the brand that is right for you, it's not about money, it's about integrity.

You need to be so passionate about your brand that you never have to sell it to anyone, you just love it so much that people are inspired to find out why for themselves.

How do you approach them?
Often you will have come into contact with the brand team long before taking on any role, but if not when applying for the job generally you will already be in the right circles to hear about it.

If you aren't up to speed with what is happening on the brand then perhaps it's not the right brand or the right time for you.

What kind and level of experience is required?
This will vary from brand to brand and region to region, it's often a case of life experience and passion.

You need the right attitude and drive, there is no formal training that can create a great brand ambassador, it's always down to the personality.

What exactly are the duties of a brand ambassador?
This also changes from company to company, ultimately in my role I am in no way attached to sales.

This keeps me free to simply spread the word, your job is to be the single most passionate person about your brand, you are the number it's number 1 fan and it's biggest stake holder.

What kind of monetary compensation range is there?
I'm totally lost here, it's completely different from person to person?
I will say it's not comparable to a banker, think along the lines of a well-paid bartender.

Hours expected?
All the time. You are the brand ambassador everything you do at work or in personal time you are accountable for, all the more reason to make 100% sure you love the brand you want to work for.

Anything to watch out for?
Travel can play havoc on a relationship, make sure you have a strong bond with your better half, I am very lucky to have a patient and supportive girlfriend.

If you are in a relationship be sure to consult your partner before applying for the job!

Do you have any good or bad stories to share about being one?
Becoming a brand ambassador is one of the best things I could have ever done, travel opens the mind, it has made me a better person and has afforded me opportunities to grow in ways I couldn't have imagined. It's also given me plenty of stories to tell my grandchildren someday.

Is there anything that I didn't ask that people should definitely know?
It's harder than it looks.

<u>Help Us Make This Book Even Better</u>

We want your help to make our Book even better! You've now got lots of things to try out and see what works for you.

We want to know which ones you try and what happens when you do.

Some are simple and some take some preparation but our goal is to create the best learning programs possible.

The way to do that is to keep it growing with real service industry professionals like you, using our suggestions and writing us to tell us what you think.

We will reward the people who really get involved and submit the best, and most comprehensive, case studies.

Tell us...

What worked?
What didn't work?
Why do you think it worked or didn't?

What did your guests say?
How did they tip?
Send us pictures if applicable.

We want to know it all.

Think of it as one big scientific experiment.

You are the beta testers.
It's easy! Just write the suggestion you tried and
Whatever happened and/or what you learned.

We would also like to know if you didn't like something or basically anything You feel like we should know so we can improve it.

Benefit To You - If we use your comments, we will be giving away free "Unlimited Access" memberships.

We will of course give full credit to any person whose comments we use.

I really, really hope you think this is an amazing book right now, but I want to continue to make it better. I want to give people the most complete picture of what it takes to become a "Truly Exceptional and Successful Service Giver in every major job title!"

What I learned when I taught my very first staff training seminar, 21 years ago, was that as successful as I was as an individual, and as good of a course that I had written and was teaching to my class....
It was still only my perspective and my experiences.

I like to think it was a good class even then, but still only one person's opinions.

If my goal is to be a great teacher, I should not only teach what I know from my years of experience, I also needed to encourage the people in the room to share their knowledge too.

That's why we've had such great success with our teaching. We know that it's not all about us. It's not all about me.

So, I really hope you'll join our team and our community. Let's help people in our industry all around the world become better at what they do
so We can ALL make more money and have more fun!

Scott Young and the entire team at…

www.NightclubBarAndRestaurantTraining.Com   www.ExtremeBartending.Com
www.TheBartendingMasters.Com   www.MixedDrinkRecipes.Net

Please Send Your Comments…
Good, bad or awesome to… Barsmart@ Extremebartending.com

Thank you again for buying our book and/or hiring us to train your staff etc…

Printed in the United States
By Bookmasters